Your Role as Primary School Subject Co-ordinator

Your Role as Primary School Subject Co-ordinator

Mary Briggs

IN ASSOCIATION WITH

TheOpen
University

Hodder & Stoughton

A MEMBER OF THE HODDER HEADLINE GROUP

British Library Cataloguing in Publication Data
A catalogue record for this title is available from the British Library

ISBN 0 340 67967 0

First published 1997
Impression number   10 9 8 7 6 5 4 3 2 1
Year   2002 2001 2000 1999 1998 1997

Typeset by Wearset, Boldon, Tyne & Wear
Printed in Great Britain for Hodder & Stoughton Educational, a division of Hodder Headline
Plc, 338 Euston Road, London NW1 3BH by Redwood Books, Trowbridge, Wiltshire.

Contents

Foreword

As Mary Briggs reminds us, it is now many decades since it was first recognised that at least some teachers in primary schools, in addition to the head teacher, should take on responsibilities beyond those of class-teaching. It is thirty years since the Plowden Report (Central Advisory Council for Education, 1967) noted that 'it is increasingly difficult for [head teachers] to be up to date with all the developments and sensible that they should invite the help of assistant teachers in preparing schemes, in giving advice to their colleagues, and in the selection of books, materials and equipment' (Paragraph 934), and that 'the main role of a consultant teacher should be advisory, but he (sic) might sometimes take over a class for part of a week' (Paragraph 937).

Over those thirty years, the pressure for the delegation of curricular leadership has grown inexorably and derives from the job that must be done by schools working with today's children living in today's circumstances. As this book shows, it is now presumed that virtually every primary-school teacher, including the newly qualified, will act as a co-ordinator in one or more aspect of the school's work. Furthermore, each of the possible tasks identified by the Plowden Council has grown in range and depth. Schemes of work, for example, are often paralleled by policy statements, and both must fit National Curriculum requirements in themselves and in relation to those prepared by other co-ordinators on the staff.

This book derives from a course prepared for the Open University and draws on a mass of material collected in association with that course. Through it we learn how many teachers, head teachers and local authority advisory services have interpreted and developed the role of the co-ordinator. Although the book is not subject-specific, the examples it uses cover many aspects of the curriculum. It is a particular strength that the book assumes that those who use it are active participants and not merely passive readers. The activities offered are directly related to the job being done and will contribute greatly to it. The book deals essentially with practicalities, which befits a subject that itself has grown from a practical response to changing circumstances.

It is undeniably true that the development of the co-ordinator's role has added to the load and complexity of primary-school teachers' work. It takes time during school hours as well as outside them, and especially so if adequate attention is given to monitoring the work through the school and to providing specialist teaching for those children – whether a class or a group – who require it. The House of Commons Education Committee's 1994 Report argued for improved funding of primary schools for just these staffing purposes and there has been positive movement in some localities during the last few years. Nevertheless, the staffing of primary schools does not yet adequately reflect the change of role. The more that teachers take on – as far as their conditions allow – the range of activities described in this book, the stronger the case will be for improved staffing and the enhancement of primary-school teachers' professional status. Additionally, and what matters most, primary schools will be better able to respond to the growing demands made upon them by modern children and their parents.

I hope that you, the active reader, will find this book as stimulating as I have.

Norman Thomas
Professor of Education, University of Hertfordshire

Acknowledgements

The author would like to acknowledge the assistance and support of her colleagues, friends and family during the writing of this book. In particular, she would like to thank Norman Thomas, Patricia Murphy, Robin Campbell, Di Harden and the teachers and advisers from Essex, Wiltshire, Hackney and Tyne and Wear LEAs.

The author and publishers would like to thank the following for permission to reproduce material in this book:

Box Church of England Primary School, Wilts.; Hindon First School, Wilts.; Loughton Combined School, Bucks.; Olney First School, Bucks.; Pitsea County Infant School, Essex; Essex Advisory and Inspection Service (EAIS), formerly known as Essex Development and Advisory Service (EDAS); Linda Christian, PE and RE co-ordinator, Essex; Lynn Churchill, science co-ordinator, Essex; Susan Deer, technology co-ordinator, Wilts.; Susan Evans, head teacher, Wilts.; Jacqueline Hambling, humanities co-ordinator, Wilts.; Ian Russell, head teacher, Wilts.

Figure 1, Newton, 1991 © *Primary Teaching Studies*; Tables 1 and 2, DES, 1978a © HMSO; Tables 3 and 4, DES, 1982a © HMSO; Figure 5, Ofsted, 1995b © HMSO. Crown copyright is reproduced with the permission of the Controller of Her Majesty's Stationery Office. Figure 4, ILEA, 1988 © AMS Educational, Woodside Trading Estate, Low Lane, Horsforth, Leeds LS18 5NY; Figure 6, Horridge, 1990 © *Modus*; Figure 14, CCW, 1991b © Curriculum Council for Wales.

Every effort has been made to obtain necessary permission with reference to copyright material. The publishers apologise if inadvertently any sources remain unacknowledged and will be glad to make the necessary arrangements at the earliest opportunity.

Introduction

What this book is about

There are many books which focus on specific subject areas and the associated role of the co-ordinator. This book looks across the curriculum areas within the primary school and at the generic skills of the co-ordinator. The rationale for this approach centres on the necessary flexibility required from primary-school teachers, who may well be responsible for a wide range of subjects during their teaching careers. There are also a number of key issues which all co-ordinators must address: for example, monitoring the teaching and learning of their subject across the entire age range of the school. In addition to this, the majority of research work looking at co-ordinators has focused on the core subjects of the curriculum.

This book is designed to provide a framework for primary-school teachers responsible for co-ordinating any area of the curriculum to enable them to explore and develop their role as co-ordinators. It is particularly relevant to teachers working in England and Wales, as it is tied into the historical and current curriculum co-ordination roles in these regions. Teachers in Scotland and Northern Ireland and indeed elsewhere will find it of less direct relevance, although the issues explored in this book may be familiar to them.

Whatever your particular context, you should be able to match the material contained in this book to suit your individual co-ordinating needs. It will enable you to plan, lead and evaluate a curriculum area, even if the role itself isn't formalised, and explores the different aspects and responsibilities inherent in the co-ordinating role. It refers to research carried out into the role of the co-ordinator and provides details of further reading for the role's subject focus. The research may not cover your subject area directly, for, as previously stated, it has concentrated on the core curriculum. In addition, this book draws upon the work of co-ordinators on Grants for Education Support and Training (GEST) funded courses across three Local Education Authorities, covering a wide range of subject areas and sizes of schools.

This is not a book that will tell you exactly what to do as a co-ordinator, as the contexts are as individual as the co-ordinators themselves. It will, however, provide you with ideas and guidance for particular aspects and the implementation of your role. After reading this book you should be in a better position to:

- understand your role as a co-ordinator;
- plan the development of your role both personally and within the structure of the school;
- reflect on your role within the planning process for your subject area and school policy, in order to organise and enhance teaching and learning;
- develop strategies to build on the understanding of other members of staff. This is achieved through offering examples, but because each context will be different you will need to choose those most appropriate to you;
- develop your interpersonal skills in order to plan and deliver within your subject area.

Keeping a notebook

You may need to keep a personal record of your work resulting from this book in a journal or notebook. This notebook will provide you with a means of reflecting on your own thoughts and actions and the responses that they engender. In this way you can engage in a process of mental dialogue which will help you to establish an explicit understanding of your own position with regard to the role of the co-ordinator. Suggestions for the reader at the end of each chapter offer activities that will direct you to record your experiences in your notebook.

Although your notebook need not be more than a series of notes or jottings, it should have at least four sections, including:

- reflection and comment based on the activities given in the study text;
- a record of practical procedures undertaken;
- an account of colleagues, responses and reactions;
- notes on your own attitudes and feelings.

Your notebook:

- document what you actually do with children and colleagues, your intentions and their responses;
- record the way in which your ideas and skills develop as you work through the material;

• provide you with evidence which can be used in appraisal when focusing on your professional development as a curriculum co-ordinator.

1

The role of the primary school co-ordinator

This chapter will give an overview of the role of the co-ordinator, firstly from an historical perspective, and then broadening to allow you to begin to reflect upon your present role as a co-ordinator.

An historical view

Prior to 1948, assistant teachers were on a single pay scale, although individual strengths and enthusiasms were, of course, always capitalised upon. From 1948, however, additional salary scales enabled schools to recognise different responsibilities by means of 'graded posts'. Then, in 1956, the pay of primary-school teachers was altered to include financial allowances, 'for teachers undertaking special responsibility, special work of an advanced character, or for other reasons which in the opinion of the Authority justify such posts' (CACE, 1967), often referred to as scales 2 and 3. Initially, these posts of responsibility were awarded for curriculum leadership. In practice, the way in which the posts were allocated was somewhat idiosyncratic. Alongside relatively supportive functions, like 'boys' games' and 'library' were a motley collection of odd jobs such as 'playground duty rota', 'stock cupboard' and the ubiquitous and highly suggestive 'display'. Though all such jobs were undoubtedly essential to the smooth running of a school, they did not require the same expertise as many other curriculum functions which sometimes went unrewarded.

This state of affairs was criticised by Plowden (CACE, 1967, para 936), but it was Her Majesty's Inspectorate (HMI) that provided the first thorough documentation. In its 1978 and 1982 surveys of primary education it identified two main areas of responsibility: organisational and curricular, as shown in Tables 1 to 4:

TABLE 1 *Percentage of primary schools having teachers with organisational responsibilities*

Responsibility	Percentage
Library	54
Infant department	41 (67a)
Remedial work	38
Resources	28
Year-group leader	16
Junior department	14 (20a)
Liaison with other schools	13
Team leader	13
Home/school liaison	12
Nursery unit	12
Needs of the very able	2
Other	41

a – percentage for combined infant/junior and first/middle schools.
Source: Department of Education and Science (DES), 1978a, p16.

TABLE 2 *Percentage of primary schools having teachers with special curricular responsibilities*

Curricular area	Percentage
Music	70
Language	51
Games	48
Mathematics	45
Craft	35
Swimming	32
Art	31
Gymnastics	25
Religious education	19
Science	17
Environmental studies	17
Drama	14
French	14
Dance	13

Source: DES, 1978a, p39.

TABLE 3 *Percentage of first schools having teachers with organisational responsibilities*

Organisational area	Percentage
Library	71
Reception	59
Remedial work	39
New teachers	36
Audio-visual	35
Team leader	33
Year leader	30
Liaison with other schools	26
Home/school liaison	22
Resources	20
Supervision of students	19
Needs of the very able	3
Nursery	3
Other	98

Source: DES, 1982a, p75.

TABLE 4 *Allocation of curricular responsibilities within 80 first schools (number of posts, not percentage of schools)*

Curricular area	Number of posts
Music	53
Languages	51
Mathematics	37
Art and craft	34
Physical education	21
General studies	17
Science	10
Drama	9
Health education	3
Religious education	3
Other	60

Source: DES, 1982a, p74.

It is worth calculating the percentages of primary and first schools which did not have members of staff responsible for major areas of work. From the surveys these were (1978/1982 primary and first school percentages): Language (49/49%), Mathematics (55/63%), Art (69/66%), Remedial work (62/62%), and the needs of the very able (98/97%). Although these examples do not cover all the curricular areas, they show the importance accorded to some of the areas in primary schools and, conversely, the lack of importance accorded to others. This does not paint an accurate picture of each school, but it does give an indication of the persistence of the 'odd-job' approach, with the high percentage of 'other' organisational responsibilities.

This is despite the changes that took place in 1971, when the teachers' salaries were given an incremental structure within each scale. Scale points were allocated to schools according to the number of pupils on the roll and their ages, and then the schools allocated scale points to teachers according to curriculum priorities and teacher strengths. These changes in the allocation of posts of responsibility led to the development of the co-ordinator and curriculum-area leaders. The 1982 survey by HMI offered a list of roles for the 'curriculum consultant':

- drawing up schemes;
- giving guidance and support to other teachers, assisting in teaching where necessary;
- assessing the effectiveness of their support by visiting classes to observe work in progress. (Source: DES, 1982a, para 8.46.)

The vast majority of curriculum consultants or co-ordinators were, and still are, class teachers holding virtually all responsibilities for their curriculum area, as well as having the main task of running a class. You may find it useful to compare your list with the one which follows.

In 1983, a Schools Curriculum Council Research and Development Group at the University of Birmingham looked at curriculum responsibility and teacher expertise in the primary school. They found that the following activities were considered the function of the teacher co-ordinator:

1. Teaching their own class new topics, teaching other classes complex topics or principles of new equipment, teaching withdrawal groups (e.g. gifted children), organising and running parents' evenings on their area
2. Drafting schemes of work, providing summaries of staff discussions, negotiating and agreeing own job specification, carrying out assessment procedures, providing a resource index, providing in-service course summaries
3. Displaying children's work with comments, monitoring accessing and use of available resources, finding out about potential new resources, attending in-service courses
4. Purchasing books, equipment and materials
5. Discussing formally in staff meetings, with LEA advisers, with headteachers, with parents; discussing informally by request or by initiative with colleagues
6. Arranging visits for children, arranging and suggesting visits for colleagues to other schools, suggesting to colleagues particular in-service training to attend

7. Evaluating children's work, evaluating children's progress, evaluating children's needs, monitoring and evaluating staff work, progress and needs

While many of these activities were included in the discussions of the groups working within the research project on the responsibilities of the co-ordinator, organising and maintaining materials were also mentioned. (Source: Adapted from Schools Council, University of Birmingham (1984).)

Although these are the general expectations of the co-ordinators of any particular curriculum area in the primary school, the growth of the leadership role is a common feature, as is the role of an in-service course tutor.

By 1986, the role of the curriculum co-ordinator was being acknowledged in the House of Commons. The Select Committee for Education, Science and Arts took evidence on the functions of the co-ordinator: What should co-ordinators do? '9.19 Many of our witnesses thought the two principal functions of co-ordinators were to advise other teachers and, occasionally, to work with children alongside their class teacher.' (Source: House of Commons Parliamentary Papers, 1985–1986, p cxxxi, Chadwyck Healey.)

Data collected (informally) during 1991 by the National Curriculum Council (NCC) indicated that curriculum co-ordinators in primary schools were carrying out some or all of the following roles:

- providing a lead in developing a whole-school policy;
- assisting colleagues to plan schemes of work;
- giving guidance/support/teaching alongside colleagues;
- continuing to develop their own expertise;
- keeping up to date with new teaching materials;
- organising and maintaining an inventory of shared resources;
- leading the review and development of assessment and record-keeping;
- liaising with LEA advisory staff and teachers from other schools, governors or school boards, and parents;
- disseminating information to other staff;
- monitoring the effectiveness of existing policy and practice. (Source: NCC, 1991.)

In the Ofsted *Handbook for the inspection of schools*, the co-ordinator is defined again: 'Co-ordinator – a teacher responsible for leading and co-ordinating the teaching and learning within a subject, curricular area or key stage . . .' (Source: Ofsted, 1993, part 6, p29.)

The latest version of the *Handbook for the inspection of nursery and primary schools* (Ofsted, 1995) took effect from April 1996, and inspections now use this as their basis. The handbook does not detail the role of the co-ordinator in the same way, yet there is still emphasis on the co-ordinator's role in monitoring the quality of teaching or learning of their subject.

Since the introduction of the National Curriculum, the range of curricular areas has actually increased, with cross-curricular themes and the demand for special needs and assessment co-ordinators. As with many roles in education, that of the co-ordinator is developing and altering according to current external demands.

Marion Stow and Derek Foxman wrote an article specifically about mathematics co-ordinators, entitled 'Mathematics co-ordination: study of practice in primary and middle schools'. (Note that this article was written in 1989 and is based on a book published in 1988.) Although this article was written before the introduction of the National Curriculum, many of the issues remain:

> *Primary schools are, at present, faced with a wide range of curriculum opportunities and responsibilities. They have been involved in defining their own curriculum policy and in implementing curriculum developments not only in mathematics, but across the range of curriculum areas. Within schools the delegation of curriculum responsibility is involving all teachers more and more in the processes of curriculum development [p7].*

You may not be responsible for mathematics, but this introduction to the research work could apply to any area of the curriculum. Stow and Foxman cite the Cockcroft Report, giving the duties of the mathematics co-ordinator as being to:

1. Prepare a scheme of work for the school in consultation with the head teacher and staff and, where possible, the schools from which the children come and to which they go.
2. Provide guidance and support to all members of staff in implementing the scheme of work, both by means of meetings and by working alongside individual teachers.
3. Organise and be responsible for purchasing within the funds made available the necessary teaching resources for mathematics, maintain an up-to-date inventory and ensure that members of staff are aware of how to use the resources which are available.
4. Monitor work in mathematics throughout the school, including methods of assessment and record-keeping.
5. Assist with the diagnosis of children's learning difficulties and with their mediation.
6. Arrange school-based in-service training (INSET) for members of staff as appropriate.
7. Maintain liaison with schools from which children come and to which they go, and also with Local Education Authority (LEA) advisory staff. (DES, 1982, Cockcroft Report, para 355.)

You may feel that some of these points are specific to mathematics, but others are common to all areas. Which issues are common to your subject area, and what are the major differences? How much has changed in your subject area since then? The scheme of work must take account of the requirements of the National Curriculum and any appropriate study units. In addition, you may feel that there is now a greater understanding of the place of assessment in the planning process and of the need to feed assessment into the scheme of work as an integral part, rather than a bolt-on extra. The other recent change is the emphasis on the LEA advisory staff; in many parts of the country the numbers of these staff have been reduced, leaving co-ordinators to develop their own strategies for support, for example, through the establishment of support groups of co-ordinators in a common area and/or by seeking support from external agencies such as professional associations.

In contrast to the well-established subject of mathematics, Douglas Newton wrote about a new role in 1991, in an article entitled 'The role of the technology co-ordinator'. The article is specifically focused on preparing for co-ordination in the new area of technology, which was established as a direct result of the National Curriculum. Technology is a relatively new subject in the primary-school curriculum and most teachers bring to it perceptions based on personal experience, including what they did in craft subjects at school themselves. This is true of many subjects that primary-school class teachers teach, since they are mainly responsible for teaching all subject areas. For such a new subject to the curriculum, those taking on the role of the co-ordinator were expected to advise colleagues with limited skills and knowledge. (The issue of specialist teaching is explored later in this chapter and at other points in the book.)

You may find it useful to note down specific issues in the light of the current National Curriculum documents and their requirements for co-ordinating your subject area. Suggestions for subject co-ordination can be found in earlier versions of non-statutory guidance and can be helpful in highlighting the issues for your subject, For example, in English the areas covered include: translating programmes of study into practice, planning schemes of work, emphasising particular aspects of programmes of study and gathering evidence of achievement.

Newton identifies two key aspects of the co-ordinator's role: support and development, as illustrated in the figure overleaf.

FIGURE 1 *Support and development*

Support	Development
Maintaining technology	Promoting technology
Advising people	Keeping informed
– about the subject	– awareness of new publications
– about teaching	– attending courses
	– professional development
Managing resources	Disseminating information
– storage	– staff development
– stock taking and ordering	– parents
Liaising with others	Preparing/updating working documents
– advisory teachers	– policy statements
– other schools	– scheme of work
– LEA inspectors and HMI	– assessment system

Source: Newton, 1991, p24.

> You may find many points of similarity with the co-ordination of your specific subject area(s). For some subjects, the introduction of the National Curriculum has involved identifying a co-ordinator for a new area. For other, previously recognised, areas of learning, it has ensured that each part of the curriculum has a co-ordinator. It may have involved planned expenditure for equipment, new book resources and/or discussion of new/different teaching and learning styles.

In 1987, teachers' pay and conditions were changed quite radically, and the scale system was abandoned in favour of a Main Professional Grade (MPG) with added allowances. Those teachers who were previously on scale 3 or above were automatically given an incentive allowance of B or above. (Those on scales on or above 3 tended to be in advisory teaching posts within authorities or in the secondary sector.) Those teachers in primary schools formerly on scale 2 did not automatically obtain any incentive allowances. This led to problems within some schools, since scale 2 posts were given to teachers taking on a major curriculum area. More recently, the terminology has been altered again, and the added allowances are now MPG plus one or two increments and in the primary school perhaps a few with plus three increments.

Obviously the co-ordinator's status in the hierarchy of the school will affect their potential influence on the teaching and learning of their subject area. Under the primary-school structure from 1956 to 1987, the status of the co-ordinator was that of either head, deputy or class teacher on scales 1, 2 or 3. Since the government's proposals for teachers' pay and conditions of employment of March 1987, every teacher may be required to take responsibility for co-ordinating a curriculum area. Although this has not changed the range of positions of status that the co-ordinator can have, it has changed the position of those teachers who previously chose not to take on the co-ordination of a curriculum area. These teachers can no longer opt out of the co-ordinator's role. In the document outlining teachers' pay and conditions, Section 12 states:

Management (12)
a) Co-ordinating or managing the work of other teachers.
b) Taking such part as may be required of them in the review, development and management of activities relating to the curriculum, organisation and pastoral functions of the school. (Source: DES, 1987.)

There is even an expectation that teachers leaving college to start their first year of teaching will be capable of co-ordinating a curriculum area. However, most heads would consider that an interest in an area would be sufficient in the first year; this would gradually develop into the full role of the curriculum co-ordinator.

This overview of the co-ordinator's role can apply to any curriculum area. Since the 1970s, reports and documents have recommended the idea of co-ordinators for specific areas. The section on the implications and recommendations of the Bullock Report (*A language for life*) on language teaching and learning for all ages states that:

Para 148. Every school should have a teacher on the staff responsible for supporting colleagues in language development and the teaching of reading. In the allocation of above-scale posts English should be given a high priority. (Source: DES, 1975, Bullock Report, p530.)

An HMSO publication about primary science recommends that:

1. The head teacher and the staff need to consider. . . . c) the organisation of the school, particularly in relation to expertise of individual teachers and the role of the science consultant or designated teacher . . . (Source: DES, 1984, Science in the primary school, p26.)

Since then, with the rise of co-ordinating posts, more areas of the curriculum have been highlighted, for example physical education (Williamson *et al*, 1984; Foster *et al*, 1987). One area which is central to the role of the co-ordinators of a number of subjects is that of teacher confidence. It is often said to co-ordinators that certain subjects need careful co-ordination, and possibly more than others, because of the lack of teacher confidence in teaching the subject area. In *Primary Science*, the journal of the Association of Science Education, Newton wrote an article in 1987 about co-ordinating science in a small primary school. She highlighted three major areas of concern of which science co-ordinators should be aware, including teacher confidence.

First, some staff might lack confidence in their own ability to teach science. Not having done any science before, they may feel they do not know what to do or where to begin. Second, science is an active process. Children have to be involved in practical activities but this often means movement, mess and noise. Some staff might find this difficult to accept, being contrary to their usual practice. Finally, they might feel incapable of organising and managing practical science. Obviously, until confidence is built and competence in managing practical science is established, support in various forms is needed. (Newton, 1987, p15.)

These issues and concerns have parallels with the roles of co-ordinators in other areas of the curriculum in the primary school.

In response to concerns about lack of teacher confidence, the following guidance was given to teachers on the introduction of the National Curriculum:

Where possible, teachers should share responsibility for curriculum leadership, including:

- *detailing schemes of work in the light of the programmes of study;*
- *working alongside colleagues;*
- *arranging school-based INSET;*
- *evaluating curriculum development;*
- *liaising with other schools;*
- *keeping 'up to date' in the particular subject;*
- *managing resources. (Source: NCC, 1989, p12.)*

Since the late 1980s, the rise in co-ordinating posts for all areas of the curriculum has been highlighted. Following the publication in 1991 of a summary of a report called *Primary Education in Leeds*, which became known as the 'Alexander Report', the government commissioned a discussion document to look at curriculum organisation and classroom practice. It was written by Alexander (a professor), Rose (Chief Inspector HMI), and Woodhead (Chief Executive of the National Curriculum Council), and became known in the educational and national press as the 'three wise men report'. It was published by the DES in 1992 and included a substantial debate on specialist teaching in the primary school.

Webb (1993) discusses the use of specialist teaching in a commissioned report for the teachers' union, ATL (Association of Teachers and Lecturers). In the sample of schools reviewed for this project, many informal exchanges of classes took place which enabled teachers to use their subject expertise with classes other than their own, and sometimes to reduce workloads. The most interesting finding was the teachers' perception of the changes:

3.6 Teachers did not view the move towards specialist teaching as bringing about changes in their teaching methods as they used whole-class teaching and various kinds of individual and group work – depending on the purpose of the lesson and the available resources. (Source: ATL, 1993, p5.)

Depending upon the age range of the school in which you teach, you may find it useful to consider specialist teaching alongside your role as a subject co-ordinator. Surprisingly, many teachers have not looked at their job description since they applied for their present post. It is an important part of your role that you understand what is required by your institution. The appraisal process gives you the opportunity to discuss changes to your job description where the expectations may be unrealistic, and to set goals for the next period between appraisal meetings. It is also a focus of Ofsted inspection as evidence of management and administration, e.g. staff job-description roles and plans for professional development. (Ofsted, 1993, part 3, p34.)

FIGURE 2 *Illustrative role specification*

Curriculum co-ordinator responsible for the development of teaching and learning throughout the year group/key stage/school with the support and co-operation of the head teacher, colleagues, governors, parents and pupils.

Curriculum aspects
Policy documentation with the appropriate links to other curriculum areas, e.g. special needs, information technology, equal opportunities, multi-cultural issues.

Devise a plan for monitoring and reviewing the policy documents.

Schemes of work, which take account of the requirements for teaching, learning and assessment of the National Curriculum, including devising differentiated schemes of work
Devise a plan for monitoring and reviewing the schemes of work.

Promote teaching and learning . . . through examples of good practice in own classroom.

Contribute to the School Development Plan with a specific reference to . . .

Monitor teaching and learning . . . throughout the school, which will include observations where appropriate.

Advise on implementation and use of teacher assessment, SATs and other appropriate forms of testing achievement.

Develop and review record-keeping, including individual profiles, records of achievement and school records of learning outcomes.

Foster the moderation of work and agreed-upon attainment reached for specific pupils and/or pieces of work.

Budget/Resources
Audit existing resources and maintain an up-to-date list of all resources and their whereabouts.

Organise appropriate storage for all resources in conjunction with colleagues using these.

Monitor the use of resources and planning, for example to promote those underused, and match to the needs of the curriculum.

Plan within the budget any constraints to purchase appropriate additional resources and devise planned expenditure for future years.

Development
Audit staff skills, interests and talents within the teaching and learning of . . .

Plan, arrange, and organise school-based in-service activities.

Plan and carry out continued professional development of self, including attendance at courses, reading and membership of appropriate professional bodies.

Act as adviser to colleagues, non-teaching and teaching staff.

Liaise with appropriate co-ordinators and others in feeder schools.

Communicate with the wider school community: parents, governors and other local groups.
Take part in any appropriate induction and mentoring of students, NQTs and other staff.

Source: **Box Church of England Primary School, Wiltshire.**

FIGURE 3 *Job Description for Main Professional Grade Teacher*

Teacher's name .... Post ....
Date of appointment to post .... Additional increments ....
Specific area(s) of responsibility ....
Signature of teacher .... Date ....

1. Introduction
1.1 This document should be read in conjunction with the School Teachers' Pay and Conditions Document 1994.
1.2 Members of staff should at all times support, and work within the framework provided by, the school's Statement of Purpose, and agreed Aims and Objectives.

2. Job purpose
2.1 To ensure the effective education of the pupils for whom you have class/group responsibility, giving attention to their development, spiritually, morally, socially, emotionally, physically, and intellectually.

2.2 To ensure continuity of policy throughout the school within the agreed areas of responsibility as listed above.

3. Key responsibilities
3.1 To the children for whom you are responsible at any one time; for effective learning and good behaviour.
3.2 To pupils and colleagues for your own professional behaviour.
3.3 To colleagues for their professional development.
3.4 To parents and pupils, to assure effective and constructive home/school liaison.
3.5 To the Head teacher and Governors of the school.

4. Key tasks
4.1 To ensure the effective education of the pupils in your care, in line with the school's Aims and Objectives, Policies and Schemes of Work.
4.2 To plan, provide and review class-based activities that lead to the effective education of the children in your charge and to endeavour to develop in them the ability to take responsibility for their own learning.
4.3 To maximise the potential of each child in all areas of his/her development.
4.4 To ensure the good behaviour of all children in your care, and to develop within them positive attitudes towards themselves, adults, peers, property and work.
4.5 To participate in agreed school assessment procedures, and maintain effective records in relation to the progress of the class and individual children.
4.6 To develop and maintain a harmonious and constructive home/school partnership.
4.7 To share in the development of positive school/community relationships.
4.8 To consult and inform parents regarding the progress, attainment and attitudes of their children.
4.9 To attend staff meetings and Teacher Development Days as directed.
4.10 To participate in arrangements for further training and the development of your own professional skills and knowledge.
4.11 To contribute to the pastoral work within the school.

5. Key tasks relating to assigned area(s) of responsibility
5.1 Curriculum design:
  i) Participate in the setting of School Aims and Objectives.
  ii) In consultation with the Senior Management Team and staff, direct the formulation, review and/or revision of written Guidelines, Policies and Schemes of Work for the given curriculum area(s) as listed above.
 iii) Ensure that each given curriculum area reflects cross-curricular concerns such as multi-cultural issues, equal opportunities and personal and social education.
 iv) Organise the integration of Information Technology/Computer Assisted Learning across the curriculum.
  v) Support teachers in their efforts to devise teaching/learning strategies that are appropriate to the full ability range.
 vi) Foster curriculum continuity, consistency, balance, match and progression throughout the whole school.
vii) Organise whole-school themes and activities relating to the given curriculum area.
viii) Contribute to the School Development Plan.

5.2 Communication. Within the given curriculum area(s):
  i) Communicate effectively within the school.

ii) Act as consultant to colleagues.
iii) Encourage positive attitudes.
iv) Inform newly appointed colleagues of school policy.
v) Communicate with the wider community, e.g. parents, governors, industry, etc.
vi) Liaise with other agencies and support services.
vii) Liaise with other phases of education.

5.3 Assessment and monitoring. Within the given curriculum area(s):
i) Assess and evaluate the delivery of the curriculum throughout the school, ensuring consistency with school policies and the National Curriculum.
ii) Assist in the process of monitoring and moderating levels of achievement within the school.
iii) Observe, on occasions, the teaching of the agreed curriculum.
iv) Oversee the development and use of agreed systems of record-keeping.
v) Advise on and support the implementation and use of agreed assessment procedures and SATs.

5.4 Resources
i) Evaluate existing resources.
ii) Manage the purchase and deployment of resources and equipment.
iii) Budget for these resources efficiently.

5.5 Professional development
i) Arrange and organise school-based activities.
ii) Keep up to date by personal reading.
iii) Attend appropriate courses and report back.

6. Other duties
6.1 Members of staff may be required from time to time to undertake other duties as directed by the head teacher.

Note: This document does not direct the particular amount of time to be spent on carrying out tasks and responsibilities and no part of it may be so construed. In allocating time to the performance of tasks and responsibilities, staff should use Directed Time in accordance with the school's current Directed Time policy and have regard to the relevant paragraphs in the School Teachers' Pay and Conditions Document 1994. *Source:* Box Church of England Primary School, Wiltshire.

At this stage, it would be a good idea to collect information on the totality of your role so that you can use this as a resource as you read through this book. You will need a copy of your job description, a copy of the staff handbook, and any other appropriate documentation. The policy of shifting curriculum co-ordination into the main responsibilities of each primary-school teacher has resulted in changes in the allocation of staff and in expectations of additional activities for teachers. Expectations will vary from school to school but these should be detailed in any job description so it is essential that you read these documents carefully.

FIGURE 4 *The developing role of the co-ordinator*

It can be helpful to consider the role of the co-ordinator in three stages.

Stage 1: Getting started as a new co-ordinator.
Stage 2: Moving on.
Stage 3: Continuing work as an established co-ordinator.

These stages and the relationships between them are illustrated in the diagram.

Continuing work for the established co-ordinator

Taking stock of present position

Drawing up/reviewing policy statement

Preparing, consulting on and implementing a new or revised scheme of work.

Evaluating progress

When your curriculum area is under or is a major item for the current school-development plan.

Moving on

Extending relationships and contacts beyond the school

Working together with colleagues

Providing further stimulus and inspiration

Getting started as a new co-ordinator

Developing good practice in your own classroom

Setting up displays and exhibitions

Talking about what is needed

Getting to know the resources in the school

Keeping colleagues informed

Reading

Attending courses

Working with colleagues

Providing/organising support and in-service training

Co-ordinating assessment procedures and record-keeping systems

Facilitating parental involvement

Promoting liaison with other schools

Maintaining contacts beyond the school

Organising, reviewing and obtaining resources

Working to achieve equality of opportunity

Whenever curriculum area is under review or when it is not a major item for the current school-development plan

Source: Adapted from ILEA, 1988.

The successor to Alexander's Leeds research, entitled: 'The curriculum organisation and classroom practice in primary schools: A follow-up report' (Department of Education, 1993a), commented on some of the effects of and reasons for the continued emphasis on curriculum co-ordination:

> *Most of the schools had curriculum co-ordinators with clearly defined roles. In a significant number of the schools, their influence on teachers' planning was evident. However, due to a lack, or poor use, of non-contact time, they were able to take little part in the monitoring of work in the classrooms. (Source: DFE, 1993, p11.)*

Figure 4 shows clearly that the role of the co-ordinator continues whether or not a particular subject area is under review or is a major part of the current school-development plan. The role doesn't stop when the school's attention isn't focused on your area. Figure 4 also looks at the role changing over time, from starting as a co-ordinator in your second year of teaching to becoming more experienced. According to the Ofsted report, *Frameworks for inspection* (1993), the effective use of resources is a key area for scrutiny. These resources include the use of curriculum co-ordinators. The school-development plan highlights the focus on curriculum and resource needs, including human resources. It should also take account of the need for co-ordinators to establish and develop their role in school as part of the plans for developing the teaching and learning of the particular subject.

Can you pick out the areas in which the work of the subject co-ordinator would have an input? You may have responsibility for resources, including a budget for these, which would clearly influence the efficiency of the school.

Within the new guidance on the inspection of nursery and primary schools (1995) there is an emphasis on reviewing the job descriptions of those holding specific responsibilities. Inspectors would expect to interview the subject co-ordinator of the subject(s) allocated to individual inspectors as part of the inspection process.

In addition the inspection of nursery and primary schools, the Ofsted handbook details oral reporting to co-ordinators and other teachers with significant responsibilities:

> *Towards the end of the inspection, oral reports on the inspection findings in particular subjects or aspects of the schools' work should be offered where appropriate to those with significant responsibilities. (Ofsted, 1995b, p31.)*

FIGURE 5 *Efficiency of the school*

Inspectors must evaluate and report on:

- the efficiency and effectiveness with which the resources made available to the school are managed, including the use made of specific grants, and the allocation and use of funds for pupils with special educational needs;
- the extent to which the school provides value for money.

Judgements should be based on the extent to which

- educational developments are supported through careful financial planning;
- effective use is made of staff, accommodation and learning resources;
- there is efficient financial control and school administration;
- the school provides value for money in terms of the educational standards achieved and quality of education provided in relation to its context and income.

Source: Ofsted, 1995b, p114.

Responsibilities can vary according to the subject co-ordinated. 'Co-ordinating technology: school perspective', by Sandra Horridge (1990), is based on one teacher's experience of being a technology co-ordinator. The emphasis is on the co-ordinator's role in the whole school, planning across curriculum. For the role of technology co-ordinator, Sandra Horridge has used a diagram to show the extent of the role (see Figure 6).

Sandra goes on to emphasise the strategic planning required by the co-ordinator, including, in this case, establishing an appropriate model of technology for the school. To be able to complete these tasks, technology must feature within the school-development plan. This is acknowledged by another co-ordinator currently working on developing technology within her own school. Susan Deer, a co-ordinator for technology in a primary school in Wiltshire, writes: 'Technology is featured in our school-development plan, and time for staff discussion was timetabled ... This is vital in the role of subject co-ordination, as is the devolution of money for resources. It helps to highlight the profile and status of the subject.'

> You may also wish to consider how the role of the co-ordinator is perceived by you, the staff, and the children. Is the co-ordinator role an integral part of your work or an additional responsibility carried out at the margins of your time? Are co-ordinators seen as the people to whom everyone goes for resources for a particular subject area? Are they seen as expert in that subject? Do they only teach that subject? (The latter often occurs with music teachers, who may work on a part-time basis.)

Co-ordinating a subject across a small school raises different issues than when carrying out this task within a large school. A small school can be easier, since there are fewer people to work with, yet it can be difficult if

FIGURE 6 *The Co-ordinator's Role*

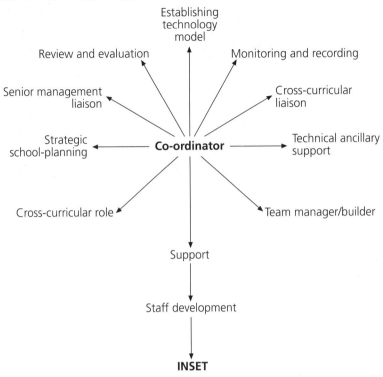

Source: Horridge, 1990, p84.

there are a number of part-time teachers and everyone has several subjects to co-ordinate. Human nature being what it is, a teacher faced with
several subjects is bound to spend more time on those in which they are
more interested, or if they have more confidence with the subject matter.
All areas must be co-ordinated, so in the small school teachers are more
likely to be responsible for subjects that they are not as comfortable with.
Another difficulty for small schools is that classes are not always
arranged in year groups, which may mean classes straddling key stages.
This in turn makes planning the schemes of work and supporting the
teaching and learning of specific subjects more complex.

In the larger schools, the number of staff can be a problem, making it
difficult to get round to see everyone or enabling everyone to feel
involved. One positive aspect is that it may be possible to have pairs of
co-ordinators working across key stages that support each other, as well
as the rest of the staff group. The larger the number of staff, the fewer
subjects one person needs to co-ordinate, so enabling greater depth spe-
cialisation and offering the possibility of utilising some subject teaching.
The likelihood of release time may also be greater within a larger school,
due to the economies of scale. To enable co-ordinators to undertake

development work, this needs to be emphasised within the school-development plan (SDP). The SDP should include awareness of the skills and experience of the co-ordinator and a clear outline of the tasks to be undertaken by both the co-ordinator and the whole staff.

Summary

At this point you should have begun to reflect on the role of the co-ordinator. You should know about its historical development. You should also know more about your own role as a co-ordinator. You should be able to see the breadth and the possibilities within the role, even if many of your objectives are not achievable at present.

In this chapter you have been asked to review your current role as co-ordinator within your school context. You should have collected together a copy of your job description and the school-development plan, as well as notes highlighting both the positive and the negative issues of your role as co-ordinator, taking particular notice of any specific National Curriculum requirements which affect your co-ordination role. In the next chapter you will begin to look closely at your subject knowledge and co-ordinator skills.

Suggestions for the reader

1. Think about your role as co-ordinator, for whatever area it may be. Jot down your list of roles and activities for the 'curriculum consultant'. Would this be different to a curriculum co-ordinator? Could you note the reasons why you feel there might be differences from the titles of the roles.

2. Note down your own position in school. Do you get release time for co-ordinator's duties if you are a class teacher? Have you ever received time to prepare for staff meetings, to draft documents for discussion, or to visit/work in other classes? Note also the number of responsibilities that you hold. How do you manage the time if you have several areas of responsibility? Time management is a big issue; you may wish to discuss this with other co-ordinators to see how they manage.

   The outcome of this activity should be a profile of your roles, responsibilities and the resources at your disposal in order to carry them out.

3. For this activity you will need to obtain a copy of your job description. All teachers should have a job description, and this should include references to any responsibilities they may have as a

co-ordinator. Although later in the text there will be a more detailed section on a specific job description for a mathematics co-ordinator, it would be useful to begin to find out about these within your school. You may have a general job description which covers a number of areas of responsibilities. Note down the areas that at this stage you would wish to review through discussion, possibly as part of your appraisal. If you are reviewing your job description or negotiating a new one, Figure 3 on page 12 may help you with the headings.

4. At the end of this chapter you may find it helpful to think about the following issues and make any appropriate notes:

   ● your thoughts about the changes in your role over time;
   ● your feelings about whether or not status matters within your school; and
   ● your views on the present role of co-ordinators, regardless of curriculum area.

   Try to pinpoint your current role as a co-ordinator. Which stage are you at now? Which are the key aspects on which you are focusing within that stage? Write them down in your notebook.
   Write down details of the specialist teaching that takes place in your school, if any, and how you are involved in this, if at all. Does specialist teaching alter the role of the co-ordinator? If so, how?

5. Consider the issues involved in co-ordinating your subject area across the school. Make some notes on the positive and negative aspects of this role in your notebook. You should try to relate the issues raised in this document to your own experience as a co-ordinator and to the links with the school-development plan.

2
Self-audit and self-evaluation

In this brief chapter you are offered ways in which to carry out a self-audit of your subject knowledge and your co-ordinator skills. To enable any change or growth to take place, it is essential to have a clear picture of the present situation, with the appropriate evaluation. The purpose of using a self-audit is to clarify the state of your role as co-ordinator, and to identify strengths on which to build, and weaknesses to be rectified. With the introduction of the National Curriculum, the demands on teachers' subject knowledge have increased. For example, algebra and data-handling were introduced into the mathematics curriculum, and periods of history that were introduced were possibly unfamiliar to many history teachers. These changes in turn influenced the way in which subject co-ordinators were viewed by colleagues. Could all teachers be expected to keep up with the curricular changes and therefore the knowledge requirements for all subjects?

The Ofsted *Handbook for the inspection of schools* details the evaluation criteria for the quality of teaching, including the following:

- *teachers have a secure knowledge and understanding of the subjects or areas they teach*
  (Ofsted, 1995, p66.)

As a co-ordinator, you should have a secure command of the subject knowledge although you should not necessarily be seen as a specialist. Part of the reason for auditing your own skills and knowledge is that this will enable you to plan for your own professional development and to be aware of those areas in which you will need to draw on support from inside and outside the school.

This chapter also introduces you to a technique for collecting information about knowledge and skills which you may wish to use with the rest of the staff to help clarify the focus of your planning for curriculum development.

FIGURE 7 *Personal audit, worked example (using art as a subject area)*

What are my areas of responsibility at school?	*Art and environmental studies though focusing on art.*
How much non-contact time do I have, and how do I use it?	*Half an hour a fortnight for display work.*
Why did I wish to review critically my role as co-ordinator?	*Because I wish to be more effective and develop the role for my own professional development.*
What are my expectations from reading this book:	
• for me personally?	*Increased knowledge and time for reflection and accreditation.*
• for me professionally?	*To develop my co-ordinator's role.*
What will my school gain from my participation in self-development?	*Hopefully a more 'effective' art co-ordinator.*
My art qualifications are:	*A degree in Fine Art.*
My most vivid memory of art from my own school days is:	*Lino printing and someone cutting their hand badly with the cutter.*
I have chosen to organise my classroom so that children . . .	*Can work on art as an integral part of the day.*
I believe that Art is . . .	*Something everyone can do.*

	Very confident	Fairly confident	Not at all confident
How do I feel about:			
allowing children to use at their own discretion a range of materials and equipment?	✓		
encouraging children to be independent and responsible for their own learning?		✓	
using art as a medium for learning?		✓	
using computers as a medium for art learning?			✓
recording and assessing children's achievements?			✓

	Very confident	Fairly confident	Not at all confident
working with others on subject activities at our own level?		✓	
working collaboratively in classrooms with school colleagues?		✓	
working with colleagues on teaching and learning on a one-to-one basis?		✓	
planning and delivering INSET in my own school?			✓

How confident do I feel about my own knowledge and understanding of the following areas of art?

AT 1 Investigating and making   *My own understanding is limited to painting. Feel very confident with making; also feel very confident with investigating.*

AT 2 Knowledge and understanding across the curriculum   *Some areas are OK, but I'm not sure about mathematics and art. The problem for me is how you make the links explicit both for other staff and for children without detracting from each of the subjects.*

_____

Now use the same set of personal audit questions for yourself, filling in your subject area where appropriate

What are my areas of responsibility at school?

How much non-contact time do I have, and how do I use it?

Why did I wish to review critically my role as co-ordinator?

What are my expectations from reading this book:
- for me personally?
- for me professionally?

What will my school gain from my
participation in self-development?

My . . . qualifications are:

My most vivid memory of . . . from my
own school days is:

I have chosen to organise my classroom so
that children . . .

I believe that . . . is . . .

	Very confident	Fairly confident	Not at all confident
How do I feel about:			
allowing children to use at their own discretion a range of materials and equipment?			
encouraging children to be independent and responsible for their own learning?			
using . . . as a medium for learning?			
using computers as a medium for . . . learning?			
recording and assessing children's achievements?			
working with others on subject activities at our own level?			
working collaboratively in classrooms with school colleagues?			
working with colleagues on teaching and learning on a one-to-one basis?			
planning and delivering INSET in my own school?			

How confident do I feel about my own knowledge and understanding of the following areas of . . . ? [Fill in your subject area and then each attainment target/strand where appropriate:]

_____
_____
_____
_____
_____
_____
_____
_____

Now the self-evaluation form; it is essential to evaluate as well as log your position with regard to subject knowledge and co-ordinator skills. Fill in the form as part of the review process.

Self-evaluation
How do you rate yourself?

	Very good	Good	Fair	Action needed

Curriculum aspects
- Formulating policy documentation
- Planning for monitoring and review of policy documents
- Devising schemes of work
- Planning for monitoring and review of schemes of work
- Promoting teaching and learning through good practice in own classroom
- Contributing to the school-development plan
- Monitoring the teaching and learning throughout the school
- Advising on the implementation of all forms of assessment and its moderation
- Devising and reviewing record-keeping in all its forms

Budget/resources aspects
- Auditing existing resources and maintenance
- Organising appropriate storage for resources
- Monitoring the use of resources
- Planning for purchases in current and future years

Development
- Self-auditing for own development
- Auditing staff skills, interests and talents
- Planning, arranging and organising school-based in-service activities

	Very good	Good	Fair	Action needed

- Planning and carrying out continued self development through attendance at courses, reading and membership of appropriate professional bodies
- Acting as adviser to all colleagues: non-teaching and teaching staff
- Liaising with the appropriate co-ordinators and other teachers in feeder schools
- Communicating with the wider school community: parents, governors and other local groups
- Taking part in any appropriate induction and mentoring of students, NQTs and other staff

Analysing your self-audit and self-evaluation

Now analyse more systematically each of the areas that you highlighted for your self-audit and your self-evaluation. What are your strengths in a) your subject knowledge and b) your co-ordinator skills? Are there areas of expertise to which you feel you have a contribution to make? Are they already taken up? You might find it helpful to 'rate' each opportunity you have for making a contribution on a scale of 1–10, where 10 represents feeling very involved, and 1 represents feeling minimally involved. You may want to note down the characteristics of each kind of interaction (e.g. supportive, challenging, conflict-ridden, etc).

- Write down any ways in which you feel 'blocked', or prevented from participating in team-planning.
- Write down any ways in which you feel 'blocked', or prevented from teaching and planning in your curriculum area.

You may find it helpful to compare your response to this activity with the response of other teachers in your school/another school. To enable you to do this, divide a piece of paper in half and use one side for 'blocked' and the other for 'unblocked'. These need not be major issues: they could include things such as not having notes from minutes on planning. Try to select four or five for each side of your paper.

One of the many tensions inherent in the subject co-ordinator is their role as a specialist teacher. This has become more of an issue with the requirements for the National Curriculum and the widening of the range of subjects which a class teacher would teach. Greater demands are placed on the subject knowledge which is needed to carry this out effectively.

Keith Morrison wrote about this issue in an article in 1985 entitled 'tensions in subject specialist teaching in the primary school'. He raised a number of issues about specialist teachers in the primary school and started by looking at the notion as being inherently ambivalent. On one side of the ideological debate are the child-centred/progressive and, on the other, the traditional/classical humanist/conservative. The former work from the basis of the child's needs and interests with an active, experimental and practical pedagogy. This ideology underpins much of the curriculum development for the primary-school years. The traditional ideology, on the other hand, stresses the introduction of the child to the shared knowledge and culture of the society, with an emphasis on subject-based teaching. This has tended to typify curriculum development in the secondary-school years. By debating the issue of subject teaching in the primary school, it is necessary to question whether or not it is appropriate to impose a secondary style of curriculum on primary-school-aged children.

Unfortunately, the composition of the National Curriculum has done much to reinforce this, for in attempting to ensure continuity and progression, it has packaged the curriculum for all age groups in subject domains. There appears to have been little debate about the effects of presenting the whole curriculum in this manner, and in many ways it reinforces Morrison's view of the secondary-school curriculum being imposed upon primary-school pupils. In keeping subjects separate it reduces the potential for an integrated view of learning, or the involvement of the whole child, which is the emphasis of primary-school education. It further reduces coherence, and fragments the experiences of the child. Morrison sees this as presenting four key issues of practical significance:

1. alerting teachers, singly or in teams, to the need for drawing clear links between subjects if they decide to venture down the path of subject teaching;
2. alerting schools moving towards subject-specialist teaching to appreciate the need for whole-team planning and discussion in devising the curriculum, in order to unify both the curriculum, and teachers' and pupils' perceptions of it;
3. avoiding planning criteria which attempt to draw together diverse items in a contrived or artificial way;
4. recognising the need for teachers to have a 'broad rather than narrow conception of "subject" specialism, a conception which allows them to be specialists in "fields" as well as "forms" of knowledge'. (Morrison, 1985, pp39–40.)

Although Morrison sees the issues as problematic, he does offer some benefits, for they 'can make for sound curriculum development – witness the recommendations of the DES, 1982, where subject specialists:

- produce guidelines and schemes of work;
- disseminate in-service information;
- lead discussions and study groups;

- work with class teachers;
- organise resources;
- teach classes other than their own.

They can also bring the twin benefits of expert knowledge with successful pedagogical experience; they lend legitimacy of disciplines and tradition to the primary curriculum, and can be seen as moves to democratic staff structures.' (Morrison, 1985, pp40–1.)

This is a brief introduction to the possible links between the role of the co-ordinator and specialist teaching, which will be discussed in more detail in Chapter 4; at this stage the issue is raised as part of the introduction to looking more closely at your role.

Summary

In this chapter you have collated information about auditing your own subject knowledge and skills as a curriculum co-ordinator. You may have shared your notes with another co-ordinator. You have also had an opportunity to think about possible sets of questions which could form ways of auditing the knowledge and skills of other staff, and will return to this in more detail in Chapter 8. Most importantly, you should now have some views on what sort of action you feel you need to take at this stage. You should concentrate on the particular aspects of your subject knowledge and co-ordinator skills that you have highlighted.

Suggestions for the reader

1. Look carefully at your answers to the questions and forms in this chapter, and note any things that you discovered about yourself and what action you now need to take.

2. Look critically at the questions used in this chapter to help you define your current position and future needs. Would you offer these questions to your colleagues? What modifications would you make, and why?

3. Try to compile your own 'self-audit' for your specific subject area following the worked examples (Figure 7, pages 22–5). You may amend this in the ways which are appropriate for your subject/context. Complete the audit and separate the areas that you wish to work on a) for your subject knowledge and b) for your co-ordinator skills.

4. Then try working on the self-evaluation sheets on pages 25–6. Highlight those parts of it that you feel are significant at present.

3
Auditing staff skills

Finding out about the staff skills in your school which are relevant to your particular subject area is a complex process. The reason for wanting to find this out is in order to plan the necessary staff-development programme for your subject.

Examples of general audits of staff skills are available from a DFE publication (1992) entitled *Guidance on audits of teaching staff*. These may be of use if you require an overview of your school's staff, but they are not subject-specific, and concentrate on areas such as years of service and qualifications. Here we are more concerned with finding and adapting those techniques which will help you to analyse the subject-specific needs of the school and its staff. In every situation involving working with colleagues, sensitivity is fundamental. It is important to value the positive things which are occurring in your subject area and to use them as a starting point for development. How do you find out what people want and/or need?

Note: At the stage of information collection, try not to make judgements and be as open and sympathetic as you can to all your colleagues. Colleagues can get worried about data collection if they are not clear about its purpose. From the outset, you will need to negotiate the purpose, process and ownership, including access, of the data that you will be collecting. You will also be required to discuss how much of the data collected will be stored, for how long, its whereabouts and who has access to the information (this is required by the Data Protection Act). One way of collecting information about staff skills is by talking to people, either formally, or informally, as follows.

Talking to people

Talk to the head

Discussions with the head will give you part of the picture; talking with the staff and children will give you different slants on the same area.

You will need the head's support for any initiatives. Get as clear a picture as you can about the potential resources available to you as the co-ordinator. For example, is class release possible in order to work alongside colleagues? Are INSET finances available for funding outside speakers, teaching resources, etc? Try to come away with a clear indication of what has been agreed, and put this in writing for the head's confirmation. It may be possible to circulate it to staff in order to keep them informed about the resource allocation, and also the way in which the head sees the subject fitting into the whole curriculum. Log the outcomes of this discussion with the head in your module notebook.

Talking with the staff

If you work in a small school, it may be possible to interview each person informally. Before doing so, it is important to have decided on which questions to ask everyone, including anyone who works directly with children in the school.

Here are a few suggestions (you should fill in your subject area):

- how do you feel about (subject) in your classroom and the school?
- how do you feel about teaching (subject)?
- where/how would you like to see changes/development in (subject)?
- how do you feel about in-service work in (subject)?

For larger staff groups, it might be easier to use a pro-forma like the one below.

FIGURE 8 *Auditing staff skills and identifying needs*

Name	....
Teaching experience	....
	....
Role in school	....
Subject courses attended	....
	....
In-school development	....
	....
Anything to stimulate interest	....
	....
Anything put you off?	....
	....
What would you like out of this?	....
	....
	....

This pro-forma has deliberately not addressed confidence or feelings, as these are very difficult for people to quantify; information about these areas would be better collected by means of personal interview.

Teaching experience is covered on the pro-forma, since experience of any one age group might colour a teacher's views. It is also helpful to be able to draw on any experiences that you might not previously have known about, for example that Mrs Jones has actually taught all ages in the school. Subject courses attended is specific to the subject area which you are co-ordinating, and is again a useful source of information.

This would only be a preliminary exercise, and you would want to follow up individual colleagues' responses with interviews based on the initial information. This would enable you to find out, for example, why Mr Smith has never attended a course in your subject area.

Using your notes from your discussions with all the staff and any pro-formas that you have used, you should now be able to compile a list of key areas. These you might take to a staff meeting or working group for a brainstorming exercise to work out a series of in-service activities in the school to enhance the teaching and learning of your subject area (see Chapter 10 for more details on running an in-service discussion). It may be possible to circulate some starting points in advance of the meeting, so that colleagues have time to think about their responses.

You will need to collect information on the views about your subject and resources, and the physical environment, in order to build up a clear picture for your school. In addition to collating the needs of staff, talk to children about their views on your subject area. (Your notes from your work on areas covered in Chapter 4 might be useful to add here when you have read the chapter.) Can you come to any decisions about how your subject area is seen by the children in your school? Again, information learned should be relayed to other staff. As you read through Chapters 4 and 5, you may like to review your notes, focusing on others' attitudes to your subject and the necessary resources for teaching and learning. At the same time as auditing the staff's and children's needs, you will have to look closely at the facilities and materials that exist within the school. Your subject area may involve equipment and could be set out as text material in the form of a scheme.

Having carried out an information-collecting exercise in order to decide what you consider are the important issues in respect of the development of the teaching and learning of your subject area, and also where you stand on these in the light of your data collection, try to draw up a list of short- and long-term goals for yourself as subject co-ordinator. At this stage they are for your use only.

Refer back to your audit of your own needs from Chapter 2 and match these against your goals as follows.

My needs	
As a teacher	As a co-ordinator

My goals	
As a teacher	As a co-ordinator

Is there a match or a mismatch?

Auditing the staff's and school's needs is a continuous process. As the school and the curriculum changes and develops, so do the needs for a particular subject area. You will often need to return to the strategies contained in this section of the module in your role as subject co-ordinator. Those offered here are the use of the pro-forma and interview and also, by drawing on activities contained in Chapter 2, the additional strategy of observation.

Constructing an action plan

Once you have reviewed the current situation and have established a need, then you are in a position to construct your initial action plan.

Harrison and Cross (1994) suggest an ABC format, as follows:

> **A**ssess the current situation
> **B**uild the need
> **C**onstruct a plan of action

Do it: evaluating what you have done

The following chapters of this book give you suggestions on how to progress through these stages in your planning and implementation of your curriculum co-ordinator's role. At this stage your action plan need not be detailed, but would establish a clear aim for your role.

Some examples include:

- getting every teacher to plan the use of computers into their teaching of my subject;
- encouraging the use of group investigative tasks;
- developing cross-curricular links for class topics;
- establishing a whole-school policy for the teaching and learning of my subject.

Before you add details to your action plan, you will need to look at the existing ways of teaching and learning your subject throughout the school, which you will be encouraged to do in the next chapter.

Summary

This chapter has introduced you to some possible strategies for auditing staff skills. You should have tried out at least one strategy: that for collecting information about your colleagues' skills. From this you should have established the needs of the staff and how you might plan to address these. Your plan might include working with colleagues, which is covered in Chapter 9: Working with colleagues and Chapter 10: Planning and running in-service.

Suggestions for the reader

1. Try to compile a staff 'audit' for your specific subject area. Complete the audit and identify the areas of concern of the whole staff and those which you have identified through monitoring.

2. See if you can discover the attitudes to your subject area of staff, parents and pupils.

3. Carry out an audit of all the resources for your subject area and their location.

4. Construct an initial action plan for your subject.

4

Levels of planning resourcing and learning in your subject

In this chapter we will take a view of planning that encompasses school and classroom organisation as well as detailed curriculum planning. You will read about the whole-school level and class teachers' planning. You will be encouraged to:

- analyse the way in which you plan;
- think about your own views of the curriculum and learning;
- consider how your own views influence your practice;
- examine the ways in which curriculum policy or guidelines affect the way you work;
- consider the different ways in which you influence colleagues' planning and practice in the subject that you co-ordinate.

Many of the activities suggested here can be carried out by you as an individual, or by you as a co-ordinator with the help of colleagues.

In the early 1990s there was governmental concern about the practical and cross-curricular nature of much teaching in primary schools. The 'three wise men report' of 1992 (referred to on page 10) urged teachers to 'review how they plan and structure the curriculum, paying particular attention to the balance of subject and topic teaching' (DES, 1992). The report also called for scrutiny in schools of:

- the balance between whole-class, group and individual teaching strategies;
- the range of specialist expertise in the school;
- the need for specialist teaching roles as well as for the traditional generalist; and
- resourcing for initial teacher training and INSET, focusing on strengthening teachers' subject expertise. (Source: DFE, 1992, pp25, 26, 42–5.)

None of the recommendations were completely new, but they focused the concerns of quality, organisation and resourcing in primary education for the early 1990s. Within this changing environment, the role, influence and expectations of the co-ordinator have also been changing.

Teachers' planning and the co-ordinator's role

No primary-school teacher can work in isolation, oblivious to the wider implications of curriculum innovations and the need to ensure progression and continuity for pupils. For individual teachers, planning for learning has become a complex challenge, taking you beyond just the responsibility for the children within your own classroom, and requiring your participation in whole-school decision-making. At the whole-school level, you should be able to play a part in planning the curriculum. The co-ordinator's role is often to support colleagues through the school's guidelines, policy document and schemes of work, in order to aid planning. They are also expected to show the effective planning of pupils' learning of their subject area through example. In some teams of teachers, the co-ordinators plan all the teams' work for their subject area and thus attempt to utilise teachers' strengths to the full.

Think about your own planning activities specifically for your subject area, and about your planning on all levels, including that of the whole school. How are the different levels of planning co-ordinated? Where are your co-ordinator skills used? At which level of planning? Different starting points can be used for planning for your particular curriculum area. Some ideas from other teachers in note form are given below to start you off.

Peter at a local farm with a year 6 class
Peter would have had to: visit the farm himself and know what the children would do and see; prepare farm trail sheets; and plan a strategy to enable the children to work in pairs or small groups.

Comment by Peter:
I would have discussed with the whole class the tasks that would be undertaken at the farm. When we arrived at the farm, I would encourage children to collect evidence in terms of drawings, words, questions and to think about how they could follow up the clues that they found using other resources.

Ambia with a year 1 class in the school, focusing on group reading
Ambia would have to decide in advance which children she would be working with in the reading group.

Comment by Ambia:
I would introduce the books for group reading and at the same time make explicit the focus for this group, in this case pausing in the text whenever we came to a full stop. I would read the book together and encourage all the children to take part in the discussion after reading.

Jane with a whole-school staff, planning for a future theme
Jane would have to decide in advance the focus for planning collaboratively with the staff.

Comment by Jane:
I would introduce the theme as a focus for planning, in this case, 'childhood'. I would ensure that National Curriculum documents or National Guidelines were available for history in particular, but with all other subject documents available as a resource.

These examples give potential starting points for discussions about planning with colleagues. You may have another starting point for planning in your school. For example, you may have developed a scheme of work particularly for your subject area. The idea is to get your colleagues talking about how they plan, and the issues that they consider important. Some colleagues, for instance, might have raised the point that only one of the examples given above relates to the National Curriculum or National Guidelines. Nor had all the possibilities within a situation been explored, e.g. Peter's farm visit. Before you can begin to develop the teaching and learning for a specific subject, you must all be aware of the attitudes and ideas around that specific subject. This influences planning and implementation of planned schemes of work. The group must explore the meanings of words used, and agree on shared meaning and understandings. Lynn Churchill, a science co-ordinator in an Essex school, wrote about the process of planning as an opportunity to influence colleagues. She demonstrates clearly the potential of the co-ordinator's role in this process:

> In our present medium- to short-term planning, I have become increasingly aware that by working closely together there are great possibilities for promoting and influencing my subject. Although I initiated a whole-staff session last year, it is through greater collaborative planning that I have been able to provide a more informal approach in supporting science investigations in other classes. I was conscious that in a more informal atmosphere staff are willing to seek guidance and support.

Another co-ordinator used a planning sheet as the basis of discussion about planning with colleagues. A blank sheet was offered to assist the planning process, such as that in Figure 9.

FIGURE 9 *A blank planning sheet as a starting point for discussion*

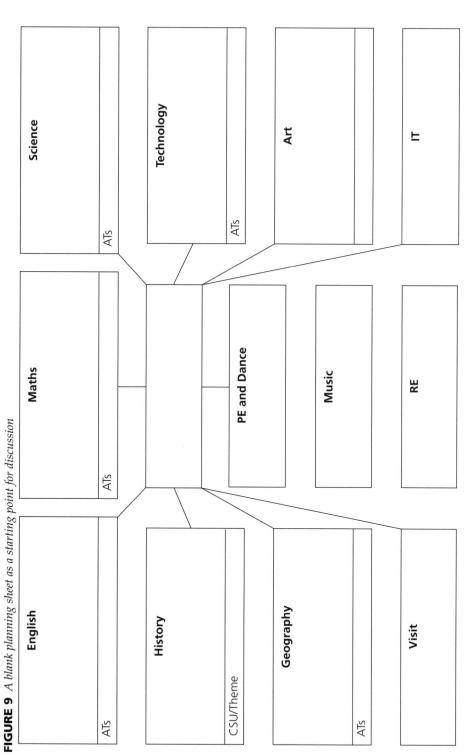

Note: AT: Attainment Target; CSU: Core Study Unit.
Source: Box Church of England Primary School, Wiltshire.

The hidden curriculum and your subject area

All aspects of the formal and informal curricula of the school or class-room carry hidden messages. These are about status, value and expectations; though they are not overt, they permeate the children's consciousness. They are conveyed through the rules and routines of the school. They are often taken for granted and are not explored.

> Think about your classroom, or about a learning environment for which you are, or have been, responsible. Consider some of the ways in which the environment and ethos of your classroom carries messages about what you value in your subject area. Think about:
>
> - the displays of children's learning;
> - the ways in which the wider community from which the children come is represented;
> - how you and other adults in the classroom talk to children and respond to their ideas;
> - how you manage groups;
> - where the resources are and who has access to them.
>
> Add to this list of evidence as you feel appropriate. To what extent do you intentionally plan for the issues above? Try to think about those that you intentionally plan for and those that you don't. If you were to use this activity with colleagues, what would you notice about the group lists?
>   Now think about your whole-school context using the same list of processes and issues.

You could use Figure 9 as a focus of staff activity as part of INSET on your particular subject area. Some curriculum areas lend themselves to display more easily than others. This can convey messages about the rel-ative importance given to a subject, or could be a purely practical issue about the transfer of work for display purposes. Physical education can be difficult to display, unless photographs or posters are used. In mathe-matics, how much work is displayed, or is it purely a question of tessel-lation (shapes that fit together with no spaces) and graphs? What message does this convey about mathematics and physical education?

Getting colleagues to work in pairs when comparing their notes from these activities would be useful in gauging the responses to specific cur-riculum areas.

Here you have considered briefly how teachers and a school's staff structure the relationships and the environment of school in order to reflect their ideas about how school ought to be. In paying attention to this value-laden context, you are recognising that the ethos of your classroom and schools is important and influential. Here are some responses from some primary-school teachers to these issues:

> **On classroom messages and values:**
> Displays: not all the results of learning can be displayed, and what the teacher chooses to display will influence what the children think the teacher or school values.
> Relationships: praise for certain types of behaviour and valuing certain of the children's interests by the teacher.
> Equipment/resources: how resources are organised; which resources are looked after carefully, etc. Children may interpret what teachers value from how resources are organised.
> **On whole-school messages and values:**
> For information on these you could review the prospectus and staff handbook, as well as the annual report to parents.

Teachers can find it valuable to talk to colleagues in other schools about how their ethos evolves, is planned and shared. Can ethos be planned, or is it facilitated? In this book we take the view that both are possible and necessary.

You may think of some of the planning that you are engaged in as routine aspects of classroom life, such as deciding when or how to take the register; talking to children about objects or experiences that they have brought to school; deciding or suggesting where individuals, pairs or groups might sit in order to work on particular tasks; sending children out to play; encouraging children to go and find the resources that they need for their learning. Much of the planning that you do at classroom organisation and management level may involve no conscious effort. Detailed curriculum planning, or planning aspects of the school's ethos, requires more conscious engagement. However, the way in which you organise teaching space and the children within it provides messages for the children about what is expected and valued in the curriculum and learning. For many teachers, organisation and management is the one aspect of their teaching that they are most reluctant to alter, implying that the values embedded in their approach are deeply held.

Resourcing learning

Resource provision and management is a major part of planning the learning environment at whole-school and classroom level, again reflecting attitudes about the nature of learning and teaching. The ways in which resources are used, and by whom, are as significant as the way in which they are organised, influencing the way in which you plan what children learn.

Resourcing learning is a whole-school issue, and thinking about the way in which shared resources are made accessible to the children and staff can tell us much about the continuity of expectations held among the staff in the school.

As a co-ordinator, resourcing is a key part of your role, especially evaluating the organisation of resources, as this enhances the effective use of resources. It also encourages the teaching and learning of your subject area, especially if scarce resources are a major issue in your school, or you are emphasising the possibilities within your subject area.

- Consider where the resources for your curriculum area are stored.
- What kind of questions would you want to ask about how their layout relates to the use of these resources by different people in the school community?
- What evidence would satisfy you about their use by different people?

If you run in-service activities for your curriculum area, resourcing will feature strongly: in terms of either reviewing current school policy or setting up new resource structures. The above questions could be modified for use by the whole staff. Are there resources of which staff are not aware? You may know this from the information that you have collected from staff, or possibly by the fact that some resources in a central store have dust on them. Why?

Centralised resources

You may have taken note of the accessibility of resources. For example, a central area may have been set up by you/other staff so that individuals (adults and children) can see at a glance where things are, what is available, what is being used, and by whom. The centralised system is a physical representation of a shared ethos and willingness to collaborate in all aspects of planning for learning in a particular school. The shared ethos includes trusting children to use, find and return resources without adult supervision.

The classroom resources

The policy may be that resources should be well labelled, stored as much as possible in subject/topic areas, and open and accessible to children. How far do you feel that this is practicable?

You might like to ask your children what they think about the organisation and accessibility of resources to see if they have any productive suggestions for improvements. What do you do, for example, with a resource like mirrors, which will be used in mathematics, science and art/design?

Financial responsibility for resources

As a co-ordinator, you may have responsibility for a budget for your curriculum area to enable you to resource learning efficiently. It will help you if you are familiar with the Ofsted inspection criteria:

7.6 (11) Resources for learning
Evaluation criteria
Learning resources are to be evaluated in terms of their effect on the standards achieved and the quality of learning in relation to their:

- *availability*
- *accessibility*
- *quality*
- *efficient use in the curriculum.*

Evidence should include:

a) inspection of available learning resources, including library provision, and access by pupils and staff to an appropriate range of books, information-technology resources, and audio and visual materials to support the curriculum;
b) spending per pupil on resources for learning, budget provision for resourcing different parts of the curriculum, and comparison with national and local levels;
c) use of out-of-school resources, such as residential facilities, educational visits and community resources, and the impact on these of the changing policy adopted by the school;
d) use made of funds raised by the school or through sponsorship;
e) relation of resource provision to the school-development plan;
f) access to specialist resources for pupils for SEN. (Source: Ofsted, 1993, part 2, pp36–7.)

Even if you do not have direct financial responsibility, you will have the opportunity to put forward a case for particular resources. You may also be asked questions by a member of an Ofsted team when they visit your school as part of the inspection process.

Children's work as a resource

A strongly held view among British primary-school teachers is that displays enhance motivation, create a positive climate about work, give feedback to the children about their efforts, and demonstrate the work that the teacher has achieved.

How far can displays also act as resources for children and parents to learn about the nature of the work that they are doing? By saving, displaying and labelling children's work, particularly for pupils new to school, teachers provide models of what they expect and value in areas of the curriculum in which school meanings do not necessarily coincide with home meanings. This will be true for parents as well as for children.

There are policies in many schools which include labelling in a number of languages. As a co-ordinator, you will be demonstrating by example either in your classroom or in displays around the school.

> As a co-ordinator of a particular curriculum area, what are your thoughts on the purpose of display areas? In demonstrating through example, what would you be emphasising to other teachers, parents and children? Would your displays emphasise the potential capabilities of children?
>
> How do you label and use displays or persuade the rest of the staff to use a similar approach in your subject?
>
> How well/how often do displays focus on your curriculum area: within the school as a whole; within your classroom; or within other classrooms?
>
> Can you influence the range of displays through exemplars of your own practice, or can they be written into the schemes of work and/or policy documents? It may not be an aspect of your subject that you have considered before, or you might have felt that it came under 'art' instead of being part of each subject.

It is possible to show aspects of teachers' subject knowledge through displays, for example in English, displays of 'genres' of writing, or diagrams of circuits in series and parallel for science.

The children's world

The child's attitudes to, and views of, particular subject areas provide important information on which to base strategies for developing teaching and learning activities. Some subjects are seen as 'boys'' or 'girls'' subjects, while others are seen as being inherently difficult, even from an early age. This subsection focuses on obtaining specific information for your subject from children in your school.

> In order to gain an insight into the children's perception of a particular subject area, and to find out how their perceptions correspond with your intentions, you may be able to use the following strategies:
>
> - ask the children to write, draw or talk about their impressions of your curriculum area;
> - ask what they like or do not like, what they do and how they learn;

> • afterwards, consider incidents where your intentions and the children's perceptions converge, and others where they diverge.
>
> What are the implications for you, as a planner of learning? Ask colleagues to carry out the same activity in their classrooms, and discuss the outcome as a group.

You may have found that your subject elicits particular attitudes from the children. Subjects like mathematics and music often elicit strong feelings, depending upon children's abilities in the subject; art often has more universal appeal. If you collect children's work from a range of ages using these suggested strategies, you could use them as a display with which to promote discussion among colleagues. This could be the starting point for issues such as gender differences, or perceptions of inherent difficulties.

What does it mean to be a learner?

As teachers, we often assume that we know how children utilise different kinds of learning. In the following questions, we will introduce several central ideas about learners and learning which inform our attitudes to how we make learning opportunities available to children.

- How do you think we learn?
- What does it mean, 'to know'?
- In what kinds of situations do you think learning happens?
- How do we know when learning takes place?
- What do you value in children's learning?

Your opinions on these questions condition the way in which you plan the broad curriculum, what and how you select for learning activities, and how you set activities up.

However you interpret learning, it involves change. Understanding what changes and how this happens is necessary to your role as a planner of learning. It is also worth remembering, however, that schools have never been the only settings in which children learn. For some children, what they have learned out of school and 'between the formal cracks' has been more meaningful in their lives. There are, of course, implications here for the kinds of information that we need to obtain from children, regarding what they know and their attitudes to learning, in order to plan effectively for progression.

Let us now turn to some school activities in which we might infer that learning is going on (leaving aside for the moment questions about how we know, and how we might prove or assess that learning).

In order to look more closely at learning in your subject area, you will need to carry out the following activities, or utilise similar strategies in order to observe and monitor colleagues' practice. This is intended to sharpen your observational skills. Observe two children in a colleague's classroom for a 15-minute period. Choose two different situations and different children, sufficiently varied to give you a range of learning. As you watch, ask yourself:

- what kinds of learning are happening here?
- where learning of the kind intended is not happening, why not?

You will need to make notes whilst you are observing to act as an aide-mémoire.

Afterwards, you will need to review your notes, in order to draw out key issues for teaching and learning in your subject area. How will you choose to feed back notes from your observation to your colleague? You may find it helpful to discuss your notes and the issues of feedback with another colleague. An example might be the issue of resourcing practical work in all classes throughout the school. Your concern might be about the pupil/teacher access to those resources – it doesn't limit the professional teaching and learning of your subject area.

You will have noticed different things and valued different aspects of the children's learning, but you were probably aware of:

- the individuality of different children's responses to the curriculum;
- the diversity, as well as commonality, of their experience as learners;
- the social aspects, as well as the individual nature of their learning;
- the fact that learning happens in contexts that are often chosen for children, as well as those that they choose themselves.

As you reflect on your observations and notes, ask yourself what relevance and value you placed on the way in which the children were relating to one another and to you or any other adults who were present. How concerned were you with how interested the children seemed to be in what they were asked to do, or had chosen to do? How much value were you placing on the task itself, whether it was, for example, a child using a dictionary, role-playing in the home corner, using a wood kit, or responding to instructions from you? And when a child was distracted or mischievous, how could you interpret this from the point of view of the social context, the task itself, the cognitive demands made on the child, and the child's own interest in, and conception of, what was required?

As observing colleagues can be a difficult activity, try to set up a situation in which you are focusing on a particular group task within the class. Note the positive aspects that you have seen, and suggest one aspect for your colleague to try to alter in a subsequent task. Influencing colleagues' practice is a very problematic area. How you go about trying to change teaching and learning styles cannot be indicated in a few lines. It depends upon many factors, including the receptiveness of colleagues to comment, and building up an atmosphere of trust. Influencing your colleagues is an aspect of the role of the co-ordinator that you will need to develop continually and we will be returning to this in Chapter 9.

Children's conceptions of learning

Earlier you asked the children for their impressions of your curriculum area. How often do you give children the opportunity to tell you how they perceive their own learning?

Focusing on your curriculum area.
If you can, observe a child for 5 minutes and, as soon as possible afterwards, talk to them about what they thought they were learning, and what they were trying to do. Plan your observation and how you will talk to the child with care, so that it is not seen as a 'test'. Remember to ask open questions, such as 'tell me about . . .' or 'how. . . ?' or 'what. . . ?', to enable the child to tell you as much as possible, rather than, answer with a simple 'yes' or 'no'.

Make notes on the outcomes of your observation. How might they affect your planning for this child?

You may wish to tape the conversation to use as material for in-service discussion, but you should recognise that the use of the cassette recorder might influence the conversations.

Children can contribute to your understanding of their learning. Talking to children is, therefore, an important precursor to planning. A study carried out by the National Primary Centre (Muschamp *et al*, 1991) found that teachers can help children to become better at self-assessment by helping them to understand:

- the learning objectives;
- the specific focus of a task;
- the kind of learning support available.

Children should, therefore, in certain contexts, know what they are supposed to know, understand, or be able to do at the end of a task. Reviewing how they experienced the task then becomes far more meaningful, and it enables both you and the child to identify what they experienced. As a result, both you and the child can readily identify what they need to concentrate on next.

The processes of planning and who it involves

Planning as a support for learning

Now you will begin to explore the ways in which your subject has to take account of children as individuals; what they know and can do, and how they perceive their learning. Clearly, the teaching of your subject must also take account of curriculum policy, or what is intended, in the short and longer term, that children should learn. The process of planning is concerned with the formulation and operation of the policy. How do you – and your school – plan?

> If you reflect on the ways in which you plan the learning for the children in your class, what do you notice? You might find helpful to focus on a specific period, such as this term. Also focus on your curriculum area. Jot down in your notebook:
>
> - the strategies you use in order to find out what children know and can do;
> - the ways in which you decide what, in the short and longer term, they should learn; what you consider to be evidence of learning;
> - how your plan is assessed and modified, and in the light of what type of outcome.

Bear in mind that, as far as this book is concerned, the end purpose is to enable you to convey ideas more effectively to your colleagues. Strategies for finding out what children know and can do include the observation of children in your class and in others, and evidence of children's thinking, understanding and skills, collated and analysed by you alone, as well as methods which invite others into the planning process. Collaborative approaches to planning activities may include drawing on a colleague's observations of the same event, or inviting children to take a more active role in reflecting on learning.

Planning as a collaborative activity

Research indicates that planning collaboratively in order to support learning is effective and important. For example, a study in the late 1980s of infant children in inner London found that communication between teachers and parents, which enabled parents to develop at home work begun in school, enhanced children's attainment (Tizard *et al*, 1988). Another study, in Haringey infant schools, found that reading levels were raised when parents were closely involved by hearing their children read on a regular and frequent basis (*ibid*). A major study carried out by the former Inner London Education Authority found that parental involvement was one of 12 key factors in junior-school effectiveness (Mortimore *et al*, 1988). Therefore, it is an area that must be considered when planning and communicating the planning of learning to parents; for example, in the form of a year-group's termly newsletter detailing the content of the term's work.

Communication is a key aspect of collaborative planning. Effective planning for the continuity of learning experiences in school needs to involve the staff working together, and there may be an inherent conflict between a dynamic curriculum, which grows to accommodate the needs and interests of learners, and a static-curriculum approach, in which all learning activities must first and foremost meet fixed requirements. Figure 10 below summarises some of these tensions.

FIGURE 10 *Tensions between dynamic- and static-curriculum approaches*

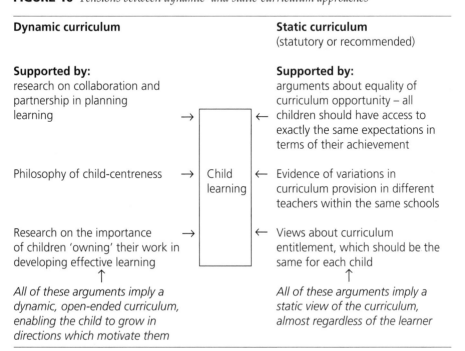

Dynamic curriculum

Static curriculum
(statutory or recommended)

Supported by:
research on collaboration and partnership in planning learning →

← **Supported by:**
arguments about equality of curriculum opportunity – all children should have access to exactly the same expectations in terms of their achievement

Philosophy of child-centreness → Child learning ← Evidence of variations in curriculum provision in different teachers within the same schools

Research on the importance of children 'owning' their work in developing effective learning →

← Views about curriculum entitlement, which should be the same for each child

All of these arguments imply a dynamic, open-ended curriculum, enabling the child to grow in directions which motivate them

All of these arguments imply a static view of the curriculum, almost regardless of the learner

Source: Open University, E624, 1993.

The tensions are often interpreted as a series of conflicting forces, pushing against each other, that are mutually incompatible. But is this really the case? The reality for schools involves aspects of both approaches. The centralised curriculum design for whatever subject in England or Wales reflects cultural and economic needs, and the entitlement of all children to have access to the same framework. But the framework does not preclude offering children opportunities to express and pursue their interests, to feel involved, and to collaborate with other children and with their teachers in planning. For within the curriculum framework teachers exercise their professional judgement in order to plan and provide for pupils' needs and interests.

> Consider the planning of activities for your subject area. To what extent does it take account of the children's needs, National Curriculum requirements, colleagues working together in collaboration, and the different levels of planning?

Planning for curriculum needs, or planning for children's needs?

So, where do you start curriculum planning? Before the inception of the National Curriculum in England, Wales and Northern Ireland, James Calderhead (1984), writing about starting points in planning, advocated analytical approaches to planning, or 'rational approaches', in which the teacher identifies clear learning aims and objectives and decides what will count as indicators of the success of these objectives. In other words, what he was advocating was planning for curriculum needs – for the knowledge that needed to be taught.

In fact, research into the way teachers plan suggests that this strategy of beginning with the broad aims and then planning detailed ways of achieving these goals is not widely used. Planning is often more informal than this. Evidence suggests that primary-school teachers spend an average of two hours a day planning, and that they tend to plan starting from what children already know and can do. Their planning is also constrained by what is available in the classroom as a learning context. In other words, the sense made by learners and the practical context for teaching has an enormous influence over the process and content of planning. Thus, on a day-to-day basis most teachers plan for children's needs as their starting point. Checking children's learning against broader curriculum plans happens less frequently: perhaps every half-term.

As you work through this book, you will come to understand that I advocate an approach which plans for both curriculum and learning needs. We will thus be challenging the notion that the dynamic and static curricula are mutually exclusive approaches, and you will be developing a deeper understanding of the ways in which you plan for, and evaluate, them.

'The history co-ordinator's tale' by Julie Davies, raises the planning issues for history. She writes of the changes brought about by the National Curriculum. This made the teaching of history mandatory, although teachers may have had little experience of teaching many of the aspects now required. History probably formed part of 'topic' teaching, though this may have been patchy. Decisions about planning have to be made at different levels. Firstly, at a global level for history: 'A strong sense of why history is being taught should pervade all curriculum planning, influencing the selection of content and methods of teaching.'

Julie Davies cites the purposes of school history listed in the Non-Statutory Guidance section:

History, Non-Statutory Guidance
1.2 There are two main aims of school history:
    i) *to help pupils develop a sense of identity through learning about the development of Britain, Europe and the world;*
    ii) *to introduce pupils to what is involved in understanding and interpreting the past.*

1.3 Other purposes follow:
- *to arouse interest in the past;*
- *to contribute to pupils' knowledge and understanding of other countries and cultures;*
- *to understand the present in the light of the past;*
- *to train the mind by disciplined study;*
- *to prepare pupils for adult life.*

She suggests these purposes are an appropriate starting point for INSET activities by a school's staff. In planning at the school level Julie used the 'statements game', from the National documents, which you can adapt to any subject. The idea is to offer groups of colleagues statements about the nature of a subject, in order to provoke debate. These should be written on cards and should include a range of statements, some upon which agreement is likely, and some which will provoke discussion because they are provocative. It is a good idea to include a few spare cards to allow groups to rewrite the statements in a form upon which they agree, or so they can add their own ideas. An alternative to this is to offer a range of statements on cards, to be sorted according to given categories, e.g. history should, history could, history can't ... and so on. The idea is to start the discussion on a subject area and to explore ideas and attitudes before planning activities for the children.

Julie Davies' article goes on to explore the 'why?' aspect of whole-school planning, suggesting the following as a rationale for this approach:

To ensure:

- *continuity within and between Key Stage 1 and Key Stage 2;*
- *progression in content, concepts, skills and attitudes from Year 1 to Year 6;*
- *balance between the various types of history: social, political, cultural and aesthetic, religious, economic, technological and scientific;*
- *balance between local, national and world history;*
- *balance between ancient and modern history;*
- *balance between the history of men, women and children, rich and poor, powerful and powerless.*

In addition:

- *to decide the timing of the core units at Key Stage 2;*
- *to prioritise the collection of resources to support these decisions;*
- *to highlight aspects of INSET provision as essential if the school is to move forward in its history provision.*

From this starting point the planning of history will move to look at the integration of assessment and the need for resources for teaching and learning history. All this is still at the whole-school level before moving to look at Key Stages, then to year groups and down to individual classes.

Think about your subject as you read the following section on levels of planning and consider which aspects of your subject are the focus at each of the levels described.

Levels of planning

As a planner and as a co-ordinator, you operate at a number of different levels in order to ensure that children's experiences of the curriculum and learning are meaningful. Figure 11, on the continuum of levels of planning in primary schools (page 52), outlines some of the different levels at which you, as a co-ordinator, should be working, and their interconnection.

Whole-school planning

When leading whole-school planning, the co-ordinator takes responsibility for pulling together, monitoring and evaluating plans for:

- continuity and coherence in curriculum provision across the whole school – including the curriculum organisation and coverage and resourcing for your subject area;
- progression in learning outcomes in your subject area;
- continuity in expectations of children's behaviour in your subject area within and outside the classroom.

It involves:

- consultation and collaboration between groups of staff;
- awareness of, and involvement in, the whole-school planning approach by all staff;
- consistent expectations of the contribution to planning which can be made by children, parents and governors.

Key-stage planning
Its function to plan and evaluate:

- continuity and coherence in curriculum provision across the key stage or phase and with other key stages, including rationales for curriculum organisation and coverage, as well as learning approaches for your subject area;
- progression in learning outcomes in your subject area;
- continuity in expectations of children's behaviour in your subject area within and outside the classroom.

It involves:

- the consultation and collaboration of all teachers involved in a key stage or phase and includes resourcing;
- structures which facilitate this kind of communication.

Year-level planning with the year that you teach
Its function to plan as an exemplar and show to other colleagues:

- a learning environment – classroom layout, grouping of children, resourcing, learning opportunities, displays for your subject area;
- learning activities for your subject;
- the timetable, if appropriate for your subject;
- the formal curriculum;
- meeting individual learning needs for your subject;
- meeting the learning needs of different groupings of children for your subject.

It involves:

- having clear aims for the curriculum and learning through the school policy or guidelines for your subject;
- monitoring what individual children are learning (through teacher assessment and other strategies), again through links between subject and assessment policies;
- collaboration with the teacher from the previous year and the next teacher, in order to communicate information on the context of

learning over the course of the year, together with other information about each child's uptake of the whole curriculum, including
social responses to school life.

There may be many reasons why your role as co-ordinator is significant
in certain areas only, including:

- your own and your colleagues' subject knowledge;
- the current position and status of your subject in the school (e.g. if
  you have reviewed your subject recently);
- your own and your colleagues' attitudes and skills in teaching your
  subject area;
- interpersonal aspects of planning (e.g. teamwork).

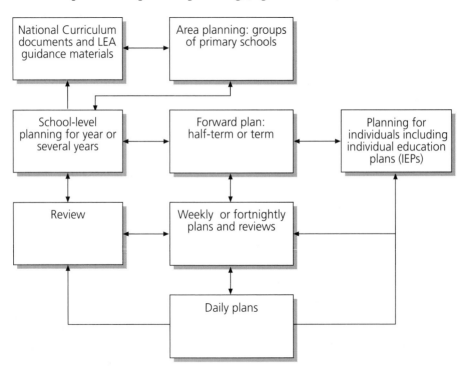

FIGURE 11 *The continuum of levels of planning in primary schools*

Each of these levels of planning produces a different sort of outcome.
Some outcomes will be found in the organisation of the physical learning
environment of the school: its classrooms, corridors, hall(s), and playground. The way in which children are organised in the classroom will
produce other kinds of outcomes of planning. Teachers' responses to the
children's uptake of your plans constitute evidence of planning in action.
Other evidence will be written or diagrammatic. At each of these levels,
you are sending out messages to the children and other teachers about

what you expect of them and thus your example can persuade/help others. Your views of what is important in your curriculum area are also embedded in your planning evidence.

As the co-ordinator for your subject area, part of your role is to have an overview of these learning outcomes.

Summary

In this chapter you have been given some activities to enable you to begin to consider the different levels of planning for your subject area. You have been asked to begin thinking about the levels at which planning takes place, and to start analysing the messages which you and your colleagues send out about your views of learning and of your subject area.

You have considered potential tension between a dynamic and a static curriculum in terms of the children's experience of your curriculum area, and have investigated the children's attitudes and views of learning your particular subject.

Starting points for working with, and observing, colleagues have been introduced to encourage you to think about this aspect of the role of the co-ordinator, and I have asked you to think about the role of the parents in your subject area.

In the next chapter, you will be asked to look at the issue of differentiation and the role of the co-ordinator.

Suggestions for the reader

1. Think of your own planning activities specifically in the context of your subject area and jot down some of your ideas about the planning process that you undertake. If you are working in a group, you may like to share your ideas. Think about your planning on all levels, including that of the whole school. How are the different levels of planning co-ordinated? Where are your co-ordinator skills used? At which level of planning? As you have read through the different levels of planning, you will have decided which apply to you and your school. Between schools, and within each school, the co-ordination of each subject may have developed at different rates and in different ways. Using the figures of tensions between dynamic- and static-curriculum approaches and the figure of the continuum of levels of planning in primary schools, try to plot where your role as co-ordinator has developed within your school with respect to levels of planning. Draw up a list of underdeveloped areas for future goal-setting as a co-ordinator.

2. If you are doing the activity with other colleagues, think about a stimulus as a starting point for planning for your particular curriculum area.

3. Write in your module notebook your level of financial responsibility for resources. Also note how you decide which resources to buy and what you feel is missing from the resources if money is available. Your responses to this activity will depend upon the working practices and policies of your institution.

4. Review and reflect upon the following areas for your subject: display, resources, and children's attitudes. Write down which messages you believed are conveyed through the school's organisation, relationships with the children and community, displays and so on. Are these part of the explicit planning of the school? Which particular messages do they convey about your subject area?

5. In this chapter we have covered activities which involve communicating with and/or involving parents. Consider your curriculum area. How are parents involved in planning? What kinds of communication about your curriculum area are sent to parents? Write down your thoughts in your notebook.

6. You are now in a position to provide more detail for your action plan, and this may be an appropriate time to discuss your plans with the head teacher and to negotiate any additional funding necessary to complete your plans.

5
Curriculum planning, continuity and differentiation

The curriculum: policy views

In this chapter we will first look at the messages carried in the formal curriculum policy for England and Wales, and will then go on to consider curriculum planning, continuity and progression more closely.

What is considered to be the essential or appropriate curriculum for children aged between five and eleven has changed over time, and varies from country to country, drawing on, and valuing, particular domains of human knowledge. The shifts in curriculum in England and Wales have themselves represented a changing formal curriculum and, as you will explore in the next activity, perhaps a changing hidden curriculum. In each country, a previously accepted definition of the whole primary-school curriculum has been superseded by another, which in both countries has become statutory.

Read both the following documents: 'The primary curriculum in England' and 'The primary curriculum in Wales in the resource material'. These documents are taken from the Open University's E624, *Planning learning in the primary curriculum*, documents 2 and 3 (1993).

The primary curriculum in England

The Education Reform Act of 1988:

places responsibility upon schools to provide a broad and balanced curriculum which:

- *promotes the spiritual, moral, cultural, mental and physical development of pupils at school and in society;*
- *prepares pupils for the opportunities, responsibilities and experiences of adult life. (National Curriculum Council, 1990a, p1.)*

FIGURE 12 *The development of the primary-school curriculum in England*

Hirst (1965) Forms of knowledge	DES (1985) Areas of experience	Education Reform Act (1988) National curriculum	National Curriculum Council (1990) Whole curriculum
mathematical knowledge	mathematical	mathematics	mathematics
physical sciences	scientific	science	science
human sciences	technological	technology	technology
history	human and social	history	history
literature/fine arts	aesthetic and creative	geography	geography
philosophy	linguistic and literary	English	English
religion	moral	(Welsh)	(Welsh)
	physical	music	music
	spiritual	art	art
		PE	PE
		+ religious education	+ religious education

key stage 1   key stage 2

cross-curricular themes

skills + dimensions

Source: Open University, E624, 1993.

The statutory National Curriculum described by the Education Reform Act of 1988, together with the whole curriculum framework proposed by the National Curriculum Council (NCC0 in 1990 for England), signify considerable shifts in the way in which the primary-school curriculum is conceived. Figure 12 shows its development.

The National Curriculum itself is strikingly similar to the sort of whole curriculum suggested by Hirst in 1965, who claimed that these 'forms of knowledge' constituted the entire range of ways used by mankind of knowing about the world. The 'areas of experience' put forward by Her Majesty's Inspectorate (HMI) in 1977 (Department of Education and Science, 1985) built on the foundation laid by Hirst. The national curriculum, however, stipulates that English, mathematics and science are the 'core' of the curriculum for children aged 5–16, implying that these domains of knowledge offer access to other domains in terms of the sorts of 'knowing' that they involve, and in the way in which children learn, and also suggests that they are more important.

The whole curriculum suggested by the NCC also gives importance to certain elements of the curriculum which were previously perhaps not as visible: the cross-curricular skills, themes and dimensions.

The cross-curricular elements

Cross-curricular elements permeate the statutory curriculum, and make significant contributions towards personal and social development. NCC distinguishes three kinds of cross-curricular elements, while at the same time recognising that 'it would be possible to construct a list of an almost infinite number of cross-curricular elements' (National Curriculum Council, 1990a, p2).

Dimensions

The cross-curricular dimensions include a commitment to providing equal opportunities and education for life for all pupils in a multi-cultural society.

Skills

The NCC identifies six 'core skills', which are transferable and can have different contexts across the whole curriculum. These are: communication, numeracy, study, problem-solving, personal and social, and information technology. The NCC 'considers it absolutely essential that these skills are fostered across the whole curriculum in a measured and planned way' (*ibid*, p3).

Themes

The five cross-curriculum themes which the NCC has identified are concerned with the social, moral, physical, sexual and vocational self, and involve the application of school knowledge and skills to the real world. They can be seen as an empowering part of the curriculum, enabling children to understand themselves and the world of which they are a part. They involve children in exploring values and beliefs, and encourage practical activities and decision-making. They are intended to develop the relationship between the individual and the community.

Economic and industrial understanding (EIU) is concerned with helping children critically to explore the nature of work (paid and unpaid) in the school and local community: rights, responsibilities and roles at work, including the role of trade unions; consumer affairs and the relationship between consumers and producers; aspects of business and community enterprise, as well as some basic economic ideas. EIU is also concerned to develop appropriate skills and attitudes (National Curriculum Council, 1990b).

Health education is concerned with the overlapping interests of individual, group and community health. It aims to offer children the opportunities and experiences which enable them to develop understanding and skills in each of these three domains. The NCC suggests that the health-education curriculum should include opportunities for children to learn about substance use and misuses; sex education; family-life education; safety; health-related exercise; nutrition; personal hygiene; environmental aspects of health education; and psychological aspects of health education (National Curriculum Council, 1990c).

Careers education and guidance is concerned with promoting five strands in children's development: the self (knowledge of self-qualities, attitudes, values, abilities, strengths, limitations, potential and needs); roles (position and expectations in relation to family, community and employment); work (application of productive effort, including paid employment and unpaid work in the community and at home); career (sequence of roles undertaken through working life and the personal success, rewards and enjoyment it brings); transition (development of qualities and skills which enable children to adjust to and cope with change, for example, self-reliance, adaptability, flexibility, decision-making, problem-solving) (National Curriculum Council, 1990d).

Environmental education is concerned with helping children to develop knowledge and understanding of natural processes in the environment in different places and times; the impact of human activities on environments, including particular environmental issues such as the greenhouse effect, acid rain and air pollution. The role and interdependence of local, national and international initiatives in planning for protection and management of the environment are also to be developed (National Curriculum Council, 1990e).

Education for citizenship is concerned with encouraging children's participation in citizenship. This involves the development of knowledge and understanding of the nature of the community, roles and relationships in a democratic society, and the nature and basis of duties, responsibilities and rights. The NCC suggests that children need to develop appropriate skills, attitudes and moral values (National Curriculum Council, 1990f).

The cross-curricular elements firstly signify a recognition that some areas and kinds of learning apply across subject boundaries. Secondly, they contribute to making the school curriculum apply to issues and affairs beyond the classroom – a 'relevant' curriculum. The NCC suggests that schools should develop for themselves ways in which the cross-curricular elements are integrated into the whole curriculum. Some 'models' are offered. Schools are advised that they could teach them through:

- the national curriculum and other subjects;
- a series of subject-based topics lasting varying periods of time;
- separate timetabling (in the case of the cross-curricular themes);
- personal and social development, separately timetabled;
- long-block timetabling (e.g. a 'sixth day' timetable, activity week).

Not all of the models are appropriate for primary schools, however; in practice, the models reflect the variety of approaches being developed in schools at the time when *Curriculum guidance 3: The whole curriculum* was being prepared. Teachers often use more than one model.

The primary curriculum in Wales

The Education Reform Act of 1988:

stipulates that the curriculum should be 'balanced and broadly based' in order that it: promotes the spiritual, moral, cultural, mental and physical development of pupils at school and in society; and prepares pupils for the opportunities, responsibilities and experiences of adult life. (Curriculum Council for Wales, 1991a, p3.)

The statutory curriculum and indeed the whole curriculum framework proposed by the Curriculum Council for Wales (CCW) consists of core and foundation subjects and religious education. It is permeated by the Curriculum Concerned with Wales (or Curriculum Cymreig) aspects of learning, cross-curricular themes, competencies and dimensions. This signifies considerable shifts in the way in which the primary-school curriculum is conceived as a holistic entity. Figure 13 (overleaf) shows its development.

FIGURE 13 *The development of the primary-school curriculum in Wales*

Hirst (1965) Forms of knowledge	DES (1985) Areas of experience	Education Reform Act (1988) National curriculum	Curriculum Council for Wales (1991) Whole curriculum (statutory and non-statutory subjects)
mathematical knowledge	mathematical	mathematics	mathematics
physical sciences	scientific	science	science
human sciences	technological	technology	technology
history	human and social	history	history
literature/fine arts	aesthetic and creative	geography	geography
philosophy	linguistic and literary	English	English
religion	moral	(Welsh)	(Welsh)
	physical	music	music
	spiritual	art	art
		PE	PE
		+ religious education	+ religious education
			[+ non-statutory subjects]
			+ extra-curricular activities]

Key stage 2 — cross-curricular dimensions — key competencies — cross-curricular themes — aspects of learning — key stage 1 — curriculum concerned within Wales

Source: Open University, E624, 1993.

Again, the national curriculum itself is very similar to the sort of whole curriculum suggested by Hirst in 1965, who claimed that these 'forms of knowledge' constituted the entire range of ways of knowing about the world used by humankind. However, the definition of English, mathematics and science in 1988 as core subjects marks a departure from the 'equal compartments' approach of Hirst.

The whole curriculum suggested by the CCW in 1991 extends the earlier views on the curriculum by attempting to show how an apparently compartmentalised curriculum can be understood in a cross-curricular way. This is discussed further under 'Aspects of learning', below.

The CCW's whole curriculum also gives values to certain elements of the curriculum which were previously perhaps not as visible, or seen as being relevant to primary-school-aged children (such as economic and industrial understanding), as well as emphasising the importance of demonstrating the cultural relevance of the curriculum to its Welsh setting.

Aspects of learning

The CCW suggests that the curriculum comprises eight broad areas of learning, which are 'inherently "cross-curricular" ', in that 'different subjects will contribute to more than one, if not several, of the defined aspects' (Curriculum Council for Wales, 1991b, p7). These aspects are:

- expressive and aesthetic;
- linguistic and literary;
- mathematical;
- physical and recreational;
- scientific;
- social and environmental;
- spiritual and moral;
- technological.

Cross-curricular themes, competences and dimensions

The CCW recommends that, if pupils are to experience a curriculum which 'genuinely promotes their personal and social development' (*ibid*, p8), the themes, competences and dimensions which they identify must be carefully planned for.

Themes

The five cross-curricular themes which the CCW identifies are important in helping pupils 'take an active and informed part of the world at large' (*ibid*, p8), and each involves particular knowledge, understanding and skills. They are:

- careers education and guidance;
- community understanding;
- economic and industrial understanding (EIU);
- environmental education;
- health education.

Aspects of the cross-curricular themes are embedded in the statutory orders of the core and foundation subjects, but the CCW has also published advisory papers on EIU and community understanding, as well as a bulletin on health education.

EIU is concerned with developing children's knowledge and understanding of the world in which they live, enabling them to make sense of economic and industrial decisions, the reasons behind them and their effects, together with appropriate skills and attitudes. The CCW suggests that EIU should enrich the relevance of the curriculum to the world beyond school, as well as creating links between different parts of the curriculum through an area of central interest. EIU should include exploration of industry and production, consumer affairs, basic economic ideas, and the economic interdependence between individuals, groups, organisations and communities. (Curriculum Council for Wales, 1990.)

Skills developed in EIU should include problem-solving; team skills; working with adults in and from the community; research, interpretation and evaluation of economic and industrial data; applying relevant knowledge and understanding to issues; making predictions; evaluating arguments; distinguishing between fact and opinion; presentation skills; and recognising the conflicts of interest which can occur in economic and industrial affairs.

Attitudes to be developed include an interest in economic and industrial affairs; a concern for the responsible use of scarce resources; sensitivity to environmental effects; and a willingness to reflect upon, question and critically examine economic and industrial decisions.

The contexts within which EIU should be developed are money-management, consumer affairs, industry, business and the world of work, economic systems, the Welsh economy, national and international economies, environmental and community issues. Clearly, some topics will enable the overlapping of contexts. Community understanding is concerned to develop children's awareness of how people relate to one another and their capacity to foster good relationships. It aims to help pupils develop positive attitudes, values and skills to participate fully in community life, along with appropriate knowledge. CCW offers a framework whereby pupils can:

- *explore their communities in a variety of ways and from a range of perspectives: geographical, historical, social, economic, political, cultural, scientific, etc., and in so doing strengthen their sense of belonging;*

- *understand and appreciate the distinctive features of community life in Wales;*
- *become aware of the other communities. (Curriculum Council for Wales, 1991a, p5.)*

There are, according to the CCW, eight headline components of community understanding, as follows: becoming a member of a community; patterns of social life; active citizenship; human rights; participation in decision-making; order, conflict and change; people, work and the distribution of resources; and values and beliefs. It is suggested that the components should be planned into integrated or thematic work in primary schools, offering specific perspectives for analysing the children's learning. The CCW recognises that community understanding inevitably deals with controversial issues, because of 'the changing nature of society, the variable composition of communities and shifts in customs and values' (*ibid*, p13).

> *Health education is concerned to develop health knowledge and understanding, to foster positive attitudes to health and to develop skills essential for a healthy lifestyle. The CCW has identified the following components of health education: substance use and misuses; sex education; family-life education; safety; health-related exercise; nutrition; personal hygiene; environmental aspects of health education; and psychological aspects of health education. (Curriculum Council for Wales, 1991c.)*

CCW envisages that the cross-curricular themes will be developed through carefully planned cross-curricular topic or thematic work in primary schools.

Competences

> *The competences are concerned with developing pupils' capabilities across the curriculum in relation to:*

- *communication (including literacy and oracy);*
- *the use of information technology;*
- *numeracy;*
- *problem-solving;*
- *studying. (Curriculum Council for Wales, 1991b, p9.)*

Dimensions

> *The cross-curricular dimensions should be at the heart of the school ethos and include:*

- *the fostering of sympathetic awareness and understanding of the cultural diversity of society;*

- *provision of equal opportunities;*
- *catering for special needs;*
- *demonstrating the cultural relevance of the curriculum to its Welsh setting. (Curriculum Council for Wales, 1991b, pp11–12.)*

The CCW planning framework

The following chart illustrates some of the relationships and interactions between elements of the whole curriculum. The domains of learning of the statutory curriculum, then, are conceived of by the CCW in a holistic framework which recognises interconnections, and overlaps between other kinds of learning and the statutory subjects.

The resource documents give a summary of the whole curriculum as defined for England or Wales (1990 and 1991), together with some indication of previous official curriculum messages.

The curriculum for any country or subject does not remain static, but reflects changes in society and developments in areas such as information technology. The curriculum, particularly in England and Wales, has been subjected to almost constant change over the past eight years. For some curriculum subjects there have been three different versions during that time.

> Think first about the structure of the formal curriculum in your country and how it has developed over time. What is now included and excluded? Do you feel that any parts of the curriculum have disappeared or have become less important in the current curriculum model? What changes, if any, has this made to the curriculum area for which you are responsible?

The purpose of the curriculum

The way in which you respond to the changing views of curriculum entitlement reflects your beliefs about the purpose of education and the relationship that learning in the primary school should have with the rest of society, including the government. The way in which you view knowledge, as well as your own theory of learning structures and of assessment, all contribute to your view of the aims and objectives of education.

Through considering your own perceptions of the national policy, you have begun to make explicit your own view of the curriculum, and of your own area of curricular responsibility.

FIGURE 14 *Aspects of learning*

Principal features	Expressive and Aesthetic	Linguistic and Literary	Mathematical	Physical and Recreational	Scientific	Social and Environmental	Spiritual and Moral	Technological
Developing	• the expression of ideas, moods, emotions in a variety of media • emotional and intellectual response to sensory experience • imagination, perception and discrimination • physical control of media **developing understanding of:** • the processes of designing, making and composing • the characteristics of different media • the relationships between arts and society	• effective communication in speaking and listening, reading and writing • enjoyment and fascination in the use of language • knowledge of languages and how they work • understanding of and response to literature and the media • the use of language as a tool for learning **developing understanding of:** • the diversity of language • the social and cultural contexts of language use • the relationships between languages	• creativity • ability to think logically and analytically • ability to use mathematics to solve problems (theoretical and practical) • ability to handle and communicate mathematical ideas and information using the language of mathematics • positive personal qualities and attitudes • appreciation of the wonder and excitement of mathematics • a sense of the power and limitations of mathematics	• knowledge and understanding of the principles of health and well-being and positive attitudes to the development and care of the human body • personal qualities related to perseverance and the pursuit of excellence; coping with success and failure and co-operating with others in individual and team activities • appreciation of the creative qualities in human movement and related skills • skills relating to specific physical and recreational activities as an important contributor to personal and social well-being	• creativity • ability to use scientific methods of enquiry in an imaginative and disciplined way • understanding of physical, biological and social phenomena in terms of scientific concepts and theories • critical awareness of the role of science in societies and cultures • balanced appreciation of the power and limitations of science as a human activity • positive personal qualities and attitudes	• a sense of: place, space and environment; time and context **developing understanding of:** • the physical environment and human influences on it • the past and its influence on the present • the human environment and the interrelatedness of individuals, groups and societies • the operation of institutions in society • the nature, causes and effects of economic and industrial activity	• feelings and convictions about the significance of human life and the world as a whole • a sense of fairness and justice • a respect for different religious convictions **developing understanding of:** • moral and ethical issues • the diversity of religions and relationships between them • the use made by religions of symbol, allegory and analogy • codes of human behaviour	• ability to apply knowledge and skills to practical tasks, operating within a range of constraints • ability to think and act imaginatively and creatively • ability to use the products of technological activity • ability to evaluate the purposes, processes and products of technology • critical awareness of the role and effects of technology in cultures and societies • positive personal qualities and attitudes
Statutory subjects which make major contributions	• art • PE • English • Welsh • music	• English • [modern foreign languages] • Welsh	• mathematics • science • technology	• art • science • music • PE	• mathematics • PE • science • RE • technology • geography	• geography • RE • history • MFL • science • English/Welsh	• English/Welsh • art • music • history • geography • RE • technology • science	all statutory subjects
Other subjects and activities	• [classics] • dance • drama • media studies	• [classics] • drama • media studies • [other languages]	• [economics business studies] • life skills	• outdoor education • life skills • rural studies • drama • dance • community work	• [social science] • [economics business studies] • drama • rural studies	• [economics business studies] • [social science] • rural studies • community work	• [classics] • [social science] • community work	• [economics business studies] • media studies • life skills • community work

[...] indicates subjects associated with secondary phase only

Themes	careers education & guidance; community understanding; economic & industrial understanding; environmental education; health education
	Some Aspects of All Themes

Competences	Expressive and Aesthetic	Linguistic and Literary	Mathematical	Physical and Recreational	Scientific	Social and Environmental	Spiritual and Moral	Technological
	• communication • information technology • problem-solving • study	• communication • information technology • problem-solving • study	• communication • information technology • numeracy • problem-solving • study	• communication • information technology • problem-solving • study	• communication • information technology • numeracy • problem-solving • study	• communication • information technology • numeracy • problem-solving • study	• communication • information technology • problem-solving • study	• communication • information technology • numeracy • problem-solving • study
Dimensions	• equality of opportunity	• cultural diversity		• special needs				• the cultural relevance of the Curriculum to its Welsh setting, Curriculum Cymreig

Source: Curriculum Council for Wales, 1991b, pp11–12.

Integration (thematic work) or discrete subjects?

In the early 1990s, politicians began to question the use of integration, i.e. of thematic work. During 1991–2, an enquiry was set up in England and Wales by Kenneth Clarke, the then Secretary of State for Education, driven by a belief that integrating learning meant lack of precision, to investigate many aspects of primary-school methodology, including curriculum organisation.

What does integration, or thematic work, mean? In practice, it has a multiplicity of meanings:

- A project providing a focus for all the areas of the curriculum which children learn about in the given time frame. For example, the theme of childhood could be planned to encompass learning activities across the curriculum.
- A way of developing skills and dimensions that is embedded in the statutory subject domains, while keeping the subjects themselves separate. Here the subjects are planned separately, but with attention paid to the links between them. For example, investigative skills could be the focus across several subjects.
- Mini-projects which integrate the cross-curricular themes. Here statutory subjects can provide a basis both for a mini-project and for exploring the appropriate cross-curricular themes.

A major, five-year study into primary-school classrooms carried out by the ORACLE research programme during the late 1970s (Galton *et al*, 1980) found that, for the majority of schools, integration was a reality, but not in the terms of the curriculum connections which we have been exploring so far. The integration which the ORACLE team identified concerned the coincidental use of time and space, so that several activities ranging across the curriculum could be carried out simultaneously in the classroom. Children were often observed sitting in groups, but otherwise working individually. Despite this, there was an intense concentration on the 'basic skills' of literacy and numeracy.

There is growing evidence (Alexander, 1991; Mortimore *et al*, 1988) that integrating, or 'coinciding', several different kinds of activity and parts of the curriculum places onerous organisational demands on teachers, and that this may not be conducive to meeting individual pupils' learning needs. The current discussion regarding this part of the planning process centres on the emphasis placed upon whole-class teaching as an underused strategy in the primary school. Whole-class teaching encourages subject teaching, as it is logistically easier to plan using this teaching strategy if focusing on one subject within the curriculum. It is possible to teach the whole class and still have a range of activities within a subject area by means of differentiation by task rather than by outcome. How will this emphasis, and that of the Ofsted inspections on assessing teachers' subject knowledge, affect the planning process? Will this lead to more subject teaching?

There are two sets of statements below. Statements, Set 1 summarise some of the reasons which have been put forward by primary-school practitioners for working in an integrated way. The integrated way is defined here as planning and teaching through activities for learners not separated into subject domains. Statements, Set 2 summarise some of the reasons which have been put forward for teaching the subjects in a separate and unrelated way.

> Read through each set, adding any of your own reasons which are not included here. Photocopy and cut up all the statements, including your own, and sort them into an order of justification which represents your own views. You may have several statements of equal significance in your ranking.
>
> If you can, talk through your ranking with a colleague.
>
> Can you identify which reasons are to do with learning, which to do with the nature of knowledge, and which to do with practical, organisational issues?
>
> Now repeat this activity, focusing on your subject area. Is there a difference in the way in which you ranked the statements?

Statements, Set 1: Reasons put forward by primary-school practitioners and commentators for working in an integrated way

- It's easier to organise the class so that several activities can take place at once; children can then move between activities with some continuity.
- Knowledge is a 'seamless web'. Learning through the practice of decontextualised skills and exercises is difficult, and can be unfruitful.
- The context for learning is not just important as a motivator, but allows children to 'make sense' of new information and ideas.
- Resources can be sought which are interlinked, instead of providing a range of resources across each subject domain.
- The displays which are created are more stimulating.
- Children don't distinguish subjects (Dearden, 1968).
- It feels creative.
- Splitting the curriculum into subjects means imposing one's own values about what should constitute curriculum subjects (Young, 1971).
- Children make their own connections between experiences. Compartmentalising experiences for them is not meaningful (Dearden, 1968).
- Children get a broader picture of a particular theme.

- If children are to learn by discovery, they need to be given the practical freedom to do so, and to rove across the subject boundaries.
- New 'subjects have emerged which are interdisciplinary and conceptually linked' (Pring, 1976) – for example, environmental studies or health education.
- Working across the curriculum enables the emphasis of learning to be skill- and process-based, rather than 'context' led.

Statements, Set 2: Reasons put forward by primary-school practitioners and commentators for working in a subject-oriented way

- It is easier to keep track of the development of the subject understanding of each child in each domain, especially if the work is kept in separate folders or books.
- Each subject has a distinct, logical structure of its own, and is recognisably different from all the others (Hirst and Peters, 1970).
- Learning by subjects enables a greater development and understanding of each domain. Progression and continuity are easier to secure.
- 'Multiple curriculum focus teaching ... (and) thematic curriculum planning and delivery ... may present teachers with problems of classroom organisation which subvert the quality of children's learning and frustrate teachers' monitoring of that teaching.' (Alexander, 1991.)
- 'In my classroom children often do mathematics for its own sake. They work on problems and puzzles which ensure consolidation and practice of basic skills.'
- English: phonic work and more formal language work need to be taught so that the children can undertake other work.
- It is impossible to learn about everything at once, so some divisions of learning must be made. The subjects have the advantage of being forged out of the experience of learners over the centuries, and are familiar to adults.

In justifying the ways in which you prefer to organise the curriculum you will also have gained an insight into your own priorities and values: those to do with learning, those to do with the nature of knowledge itself, and those to do with the practical organisation of the classroom. Now consider your practice, or, if you are not currently responsible for a class, your previous practice. Must there be an exclusive approach, or might both have a place, even within the same class? Do your intentions match what you do? What are the implications for your role as co-ordinator? To what extent are you able to acknowledge the curriculum models used by other staff, in so far as this affects the teaching of your curriculum area? Are there other reasons for some subjects being taught in particular way, such as the confidence of the teacher, or the appropriateness or availability of resources?

Specialist teaching

Keith Morrison (1985a), in his article 'Tensions in subject specialist teaching in the primary school', looked at the increasing use of subject teaching. How do the views of subject teaching versus an integrated approach affect your views on the organisation of curriculum planning in your school? You may find that the use of published material often influences the separation of a subject from others. If scheme materials are used, this tends to be in isolation. It is possible to integrate scheme materials into a school scheme and still retain integration, but this requires a great deal of work in order to produce an effective and satisfactory result.

You may feel that you can justify teaching your subject in a particular way. How do you think this accords with your colleagues' views? How would you find out? You may find that there are some subject areas that colleagues would prefer not to have to teach! On a personal note, I did a swap with a colleague in one school in which she took the music lessons for two classes and I happily took the classes for physical education. My capabilities with music are limited, especially with singing; I have limited confidence in teaching this subject, whereas I feel more confident with physical education. My colleague felt that she lacked confidence and competence in teaching physical education, thus making for an ideal exchange. The swap was an informal arrangement, agreed by the head, which had the benefit of teacher enthusiasm during both sets of lessons, and afforded us both a small amount of release time.

Can primary-school teachers remain enthusiastic about all subject areas? Can they also be expected to have the same level of subject knowledge across the whole curriculum? The historical basis of primary-school education sometimes means that teachers hold on to the concept of the class teacher as the ideal model for the teaching base. Changes in the curriculum and demands upon teachers make the timing right for a review of this model, for all ages of primary-school children. This is not to say that the class-teacher model must be abandoned, but it is possible to arrange the teacher–pupil ratios differently, according to age and subject area. For example, reading activities with the youngest children are more effective if the groupings are smaller, whereas writing activities with older primary-school children can be taught in larger groups.

Specialist teaching doesn't have to be concentrated in the upper-primary-school years. You may not have thought about using your own, or other co-ordinator's, expertise in this way before. It is worth exploring this with your colleagues, especially the head, who obviously has the overall responsibility for staffing allocations. Are support teachers used only for supporting special needs? Is time allocated to allow co-ordinators to work with colleagues in a variety of ways in order to alter the groupings for teaching particular subjects?

Morrison argues that subject specialism, combined with the 'child as the touchstone' view, can enable stimulating, in-depth dynamic learning whilst also recognising a sense of problems and dangers. One of the potential difficulties is enabling the voyage of discovery, which is more possible in integrated teaching and learning systems. In practice, primary-school teachers still have a great deal of autonomy in their teaching style, which may mean that it is difficult to have a uniform curricular view throughout the school.

In 'Primary specialism' Mary Thornton deals with the potential conflicts between primary-school teaching, with particular emphasis on the early years, and the introduction of the National Curriculum, which is organised in subject domains. From the research undertaken across 22 primary schools, focusing on the planning of the curriculum, the evidence she collected through interviews of teachers showed separate teaching of mathematics, English and science, and a gap between the ideology and practice of primary-school education. Most teachers expressed a willingness to accept advice and support from a subject specialist who had substantial primary-school experience, but wished to retain the class-teacher model. The attitudes of head teachers were slightly different, and indicated differential needs according to age group taught. One infant-school head teacher was quoted as saying, 'At infant level I think a good class teacher comes first and foremost, always, and I would forego all sorts of specialist to have the right people ... But I think, what is going to happen in the future with the National Curriculum, yes? ... we do need (subject) specialists.' (Thornton, 1990, p35.)

Mary goes on to show that whilst some of the posts of responsibility in the schools researched reflected the post-holders' specific training and/or INSET qualifications, many did not. In many cases, claims to special expertise were based on long experience or personal interest. Occasionally a post had been taken by teachers precisely because they perceived a gap in the breadth of their knowledge. The main finding appeared to be that the majority of teachers would be happy with specialist input, only if it was alongside that of the class teachers. The few teachers who saw a role for more specialist teaching, including taking over from the class teacher, felt this could only be in special circumstances, and only for some subjects, and provided there was not too much of it. The teachers involved in this research held differing conceptions of the specialist teacher, which included: a specialist 'coping with everything', specialists in the age range taught, and specialists 'in children, not subjects'. The teachers saw themselves as being predominantly primary-school specialists, and although acknowledging that subject specialism exists, regarding it as secondary, and part of a focus of professional identity. These teachers did not want specialist teaching to increase, but would have welcomed support from colleagues in and outside their school.

For teachers who have recently finished their initial teacher training, the current criteria expect 50% of the course to be based on a specialism. What effect will the changes in training, and the emphasis on subject knowledge in the Ofsted inspection process, have on the nature of primary-school education?

The issue of specialist teaching in the primary school has been the subject of evidence heard at Parliamentary Select Committees, with the following being recorded:

> *9.27 All of these arrangements occur in primary schools and some have done for many years. The late Mr Elsmore, HMI, said that primary schools have always practised a degree of specialist teaching, mainly for music and physical education. When they are treated in this way, these subjects are usually taken with the whole class and away from the class teacher. The IAPs and others mentioned specialist teaching for children requiring remedial teaching, or enrichment, both of which are commonly arranged for a group of children from a class; as is instrumental tuition by a peripatetic music teacher. Two aspects of the curriculum that we were told were particularly troublesome to some teachers are science and mathematics, and perhaps older primary-school children in the classes of these teachers would benefit rather than lose if these subjects were more often taught by the relevant co-ordinators. There is no good reason to suppose that a teacher in difficulty with some aspect of mathematics or science will be in difficulty with all, and no reason to arrange teaching by the co-ordinator for those parts of the subject in which the class teacher is competent. Any changes of practice should be decided wholly on grounds of general effectiveness. We do not regard the discussion of specialist or non-specialist teaching to be concerned with principles. (Source: House of Commons Parliamentary Papers, 1985–6, para 9.27, pCXXXIII.)*

The issue raised later in the proceedings of the Select Committee focused on the use of the co-ordinator to provide the specialist teaching, and the potentially adverse effects on that teacher's class within a primary school.

If you teach in a junior or middle school, you may see distinct advantages for specialist teaching at the upper age range. You may see distinct disadvantages if you teach in the early years. You may also have considered the effects on the co-ordinator's class, or on the continuity of experience for the children. Your views will also depend on the subject for which you are responsible and your present working context. You may also find it useful to compare your notes with a co-ordinator of another subject area within your institution, and for the same subject at another institution.

We will end our discussion of the issue of specialist teaching with the following statement of evidence that the Ofsted inspection process will be looking for in schools.

Staffing – the availability and deployment of teachers (particular attention should be paid to the deployment of any non-specialist teachers of the subject and to the nature of support they receive); there should be an evaluative comment on the quality of subject guidance and in-service training provided for all teachers of the subject and the contribution made by support staff. (Source: Ofsted, 1993, part 4, p23.)

What is being looked for here is not specialist teaching, but the appropriate support for any teacher teaching a subject. This is a key aspect of the role of the subject co-ordinator with, in turn, the head teacher's support.

Even if specialist teaching does not increase in primary schools, it is clear from Ofsted (1995) that the focus in the post-Dearing period of curriculum stability is moving from the 'what' of the curriculum content to the 'how' of teaching methods. This includes the thorny issue of the use of whole-class teaching.

> Think about the way in which you organise learning in your own classroom, choosing a day on which to focus in advance. At the end of your chosen day, reflect on the parts of the curriculum which children were learning about and through which methods.
>
> - Which parts of the curriculum were being taught through, or alongside, others and which separately?
> - Can you justify the way in which you or your colleague chose to organise learning in this way?
>
> You might find it helpful to use a chart to note down the different parts of the curriculum which were involved in each activity. Figure 15 is an adapted version of a table suggested by Andrew Pollard and Sara Tann (1987), and was originally developed by Robin Alexander (1984).

You may have noticed a difference between your perception and your practice. In two recent studies (Galton *et al*, 1980; Bennett and Kell, 1989), the researchers found that there was often a discrepancy between what teachers described themselves as doing (integrating the curriculum) and what was actually happening (very little was actually integrated). This is a key issue for a subject co-ordinator in supporting other colleagues. The type of support given may be different if teaching is not integrated. If it is integrated, then two or more co-ordinators might work together to establish the appropriate support for colleagues.

It can be rewarding to talk to your children about the way in which you organise learning, to see if your intentions are (1) realised, (2) understood, and (3) valued by them. One of the findings of research noted here (Alexander, 1991; Mortimore *et al*, 1988) has been that work in primary-school classrooms often does not offer children a sufficient challenge. This appeared to be due, in part, to the task set, and also to the quality of

THE STARTING POINT OF OUR HISTORY THIS TERM			
Visit to local museum to look at local history section in particular, to tie in with our history this term looking at 50s and 60s era. We were interested in two kitchens set up there and an old shop.			Stimulus/activity
	EIU	General discussion and writing about the visit, descriptive writing on artefacts and poems.	English
	Health ed.	A look at old money and the till in the shop; Comparisons of old and new money.	Maths
	Careers		Science
Road-safety aspect. A chance to test out what we had learnt the previous term when we had sessions with our Road Safety Officer. Behaviour in the street - considering other pedestrians.	Environment	Designing and constructing a 'room' – old or modern – in a shoe box or similar.	Technology
	Citizenship	Main reason for visit to gain better knowledge of what life was like in days gone by. We want to look at clothes and fashions in the 1950s and 1960s.	History
	Skills (say which)	The journey to museum on foot - directions left/right - distance near/far.	Geography
	Dimensions (say which)	Listening to music from the charts of the 1950s, 1960s comparing them to today's chart-toppers.	Music
		Close observation work on artefacts. Needlework stimulated by these.	Art
			RE

FIGURE 15 *Different parts of the curriculum involved in a museum visit*

Source: Adapted from Pollard and Tann (1987) and cited in Open University, E624, 1993, p39, Figure 7.

teacher–pupil interaction and the way in which learning was organised in the classroom. Mortimore's research suggested that the depth of pupil learning was reduced in those classrooms studied when there were too many curricular areas and different kinds of activities focused on simultaneously.

Experience shows that some subjects (such as PE, RE and music) are seldom integrated, either into other subjects or into cross-curricular projects. Others, such as mathematics, are taught as a discrete subject, although practical mathematics is sometimes integrated into cross-curricular projects. Subjects such as English and art often permeate throughout each topic, although they are also often taught as separate subjects – for example, in story time and art/craft lessons. Other subjects, such as history, geography, science and technology, often form the focus of cross-curricular project work, though one or the other may predominate. What is important, however, is how the arrangement translates into practice, and how you manage to stimulate and stretch children across the curriculum in a way which is meaningful to them.

Planning: monitoring and reviewing

Completing reviews of your plans for your subject area is an essential part of monitoring both what you and your colleagues are providing and what children are experiencing, although you may not be recording what children are actually learning thereby. A review may begin orally – perhaps by talking with a colleague. At a later stage, it may be written down.

Some schools review by means of written prose. Figures 16 and 17 on pages 75–6 are an example of a weekly planning and review summary carried out by Huw Jones, the deputy head teacher at Llandindrod Wells Primary School in Wales.

These plans are quite personal and potentially difficult to interpret. For instance, one group of children write stories. Do we have enough information of the language and reading experienced by the other children?

Differentiation

In planning for your pupils you will need to take account of their differing levels of ability or experience, known as 'differentiation'. Historically, differentiation has been seen in many different ways, including as:

- providing separate schooling for pupils with particular abilities or disabilities (Norwich, 1990);
- streaming according to ability (Lacey, 1970);

FIGURE 16 *Weekly planning and organisation sheet*

	WEEKLY PLANNING AND ORGANISATION
	This week's planning and organisation will centre around Enterprise Week, in which the class will endeavour to produce somewhere in the region of 200 ring binders, following an industrial process. All materials – card, glue, rivets, mechanisms and paper – have been supplied by Selter and Durward. Mr B Jones, who is the machine-shop manager, will assist us. Other members of the company will also visit.
Mathematics	A high level of accuracy of measurement is required if the process is to be successful. A group must measure 1 1/2 mm from either edge of the card and score a straight line at a right angle for the spine using a set square. The corners on the outside cover have to be franked for mitring. The width at the corner must be no more than 40 mm. The paper to fit the files must be cut precisely to 15 cm x 13 cm.
Language & reading	There will be one group of children who have been chosen to be the authors and illustrators. They will write stories for specific age groups and prepare them for the files. One child has decided to type the stories and will bring in her own typewriter. The stories will then be trialled in different classes.
Investigative skills	Most of the investigative work has been conducted prior to production but during the process the children will be asked to determine when different outside and inside lining papers should be used and of which type i.e. laminated or rough. Does it make a difference when glueing? If the card is wet will the paper stick? Will laminate stretch? etc.
Practical skills	Scoring - the spines have to be scored at a set depth and not cut through. Glueing - an even spread of glue must be achieved or bubbles will appear when the paper is applied. Riveting - holes measured for rivets and punched, the mechanisms placed and rivets spliced and hammered. Measuring and accurate cutting using the paper cutters.
Social/moral environmental studies	A high degree of group interaction is necessary. Each supervisor will check for quality of materials on arrival at his/her group and return them with an explanation first. The end product from each group will also be checked and sent on. The children must be able to co-operate with each other or targets will not be met.
Creativity	Creative activities are linked in with the story writing in preparation for the story books. The children will have researched story books for different age groups and looked at writing styles. They will then create their own, bearing in mind everything they have read.
PE/games	Swimming, cricket and rounders.

Source: Open University, E624, 1993, p68, Figure 11a.

FIGURE 17 Weekly summary sheet

	WEEKLY SUMMARY W.E. 6/7/90 CHANGES/COMMENTS	ATs levels and statements
Mathematics	A high degree of accuracy of measurement was achieved, after a few of the first attempts were rejected by another group. The paper was most difficult to measure and so the children decided to make a template, each 15 x 13 cm.	Mathematics: AT2 level 4b AT3 level 3 AT8 level 3ab, level 4a
Language & reading	Carly completed four story books entitled "The Frog and the Sugar Tree" and Rachel completed two; one football factfile by the boys. The stories were of excellent quality and content and were also beautifully illustrated. I decided to send the children to Bases 1 and 2 in order to trial the stories with the children. They were so successful that the staff have bought class copies and I have three for the school library.	Science: AT5 level 4a AT6 level 2a, level 3a, level 4ab
Investigative skills	Marked differences were discovered in the quality of the paper: Some would not stretch and split on the spine. Non-laminated paper – we were not able to wash off excess glue. If the card was too wet the paper would not stick - it was too porous.	English: AT1 level 2a, level 3a, level 5d
Practical skills	At first the scoring group did not score the card deeply enough and the paper tore slightly at the edges, making it difficult to glue. A very high standard was achieved by the end of the week. The mechanism group perfected the riveting, with which Mr John Evans from Selter and Durward was most impressed.	AT2 level 3e AT3 level 3c, level 4ab, level 5a, level 6a (Carly & Rachel)
Social/moral environmental studies	The class interacted superbly well during the week, often explaining to each other why materials passed on to them were being rejected, and each group accepted the criticisms made. The children realised in a practical way how they were totally interdependent when one area of the process would break down, or too much pressure was applied. A sense of pride in their work was achieved with the end product. The children were almost seeking perfection every time at the end of the day.	AT5 level 5abc, level 6d (Carly, Rachel, Gareth & Mark - use of typewriter)
Creativity		Technology AT1 level 3 3a AT3 level 2 2c, level 3 3c, level 4 4c, level 5 5c
PE/games	There were no PE activities this week.	AT4 level 2 2a, level 3 3a 3b
	This was a very worthwhile week enjoyed by all, 250 files produced in the week.	

Source: Open University, E624, 1993, p69, Figure 11b.

- providing alternative curricula for those with special educational needs (Brennan, 1985);
- necessary for the integration of those with special educational needs (Swann, 1988);
- the process by which curricular objectives, teaching methods, resources and learning activities are planned to cater for the needs of individual pupils (NCC, 1991);
- the matching of work to the abilities of individual children so that they are stretched, but still achieve success (NCC, 1993).

Differentiation is considered by many to be a new idea, yet teachers have always undertaken this task as part of their teaching. It involves matching teaching and learning in order to enable pupils to progress through all aspects of the curriculum. The ways in which they have achieved this in their classroom have varied. The definitions offered above concentrate on those pupils with special needs yet, as we all know, any class contains pupils with a range of abilities, aptitudes and attitudes. So differentiation is not exclusively for those with special needs, but is:

- the process whereby teachers meet the need for progress through the curriculum by selecting appropriate teaching methods to match an individual child's learning strategies within a group situation (Visser, 1993);
- the process of identifying, with each learner, the most effective strategies for achieving agreed targets (Weston, 1992);
- a strategy which enables teachers to approach the ideal of a person-to-person encounter in a situation in which resources are constrained, the unlearned many and the wise over-stretched by the diversity of demands put upon them (BELB, 1990);
- the identification of, and effective provision for, a range of abilities in one classroom, such that pupils in a particular class need not study the same things at the same pace and in the same way at all times (The Scottish Office, in Simpson, 1989);
- the separation and ranking of students to a multiple set of criteria (Lacey, 1970).

Differentiation is more important now as a result of the entitlement curriculum. Pupils must have access to a broad and balanced curriculum, delivered in an appropriately differentiated manner, enabling progression and continuity. However the pupils are grouped, there will be a diversity in their learning and in their characteristics. Recognising this diversity of need lies at the core of differentiation. Your school may have a separate policy on differentiation and/or the issue may be integrated into each of the subject policies.

Differentiation can be achieved by:

- task – that is, children are given different tasks to undertake;
- interest – that is, linked to task by utilising the children's individual interests, perhaps within a topic or specific activity;
- outcome – that is, children are given the same task but the expectation of outcome is different;
- forms of support – that is, the organisation of support to enable children to undertake a task e.g. a reading game with welfare-assistant support;
- grouping – that is, grouping children to enable them to undertake a task and to provide modelling e.g. mixed-ability grouping for a collaborative piece of writing or a group of similar-ability children providing support within the group.

Initiating discussion about differentiation, focusing on your subject with your colleagues can be difficult. One way of starting is to use a version of the 'cards' activity from Chapter 4. Either start with a set of statements, of the form 'differentiation is . . .' and ask the group to sort these into those that they agree with and those they disagree with. Or use a set of cards saying things like 'meets everyone's needs', and ask the group to sort them according to categories like 'differentiation must', 'differentiation can', 'differentiation cannot' . . . etc. This method can be used to elicit colleagues' views of the issue, and can give you insights into the various ways of working within your subject.

Ensuring differentiation requires a systematic and effective use of resources. Appropriate resources are essential in order to facilitate differentiation, and should include the assessment for your subject. Investigative work has been one way of matching child with task, differentiating by task or outcome.

Investigative, enquiry-based work requires a good supply of the appropriate resources. The HMI report on mathematics in primary schools found that the majority of children were working from work cards rather than with apparatus and that, particularly as the children moved up the primary school, resources for investigative work became more skimped. HMI pointed out that juniors and able children need to work with resources as much as the younger infants and lower attainers. For many schools, resourcing is inadequate because of a shortage of funds, but some deficiencies could be met without great cost by thinking through priorities and needs and making different choices about where funds should be allocated (DES, 1989b).

Realistically, as Pollard points out, task match does not happen in a social vacuum:

- teachers and children adapt to their classroom life together and their social strategies often mesh to produce sets of stable, routine practices which are understood and used to 'cope' with the situation;

- if teachers regularly give work that pupils perceive as 'too hard' or take no account of friendships and the social atmosphere, the work set is likely to be regarded as unfair and the pupil's motivation will be reduced. A task should thus be socially as well as cognitively appropriate. Both types of matching are necessary if children are to apply themselves fully to learning, and each is insufficient on its own. (Source: Pollard, 1985, pp5–7.)

This is an interesting and realistic reflection, and should not be forgotten when we consider the learning purposes of such activities and how they might be categorised.

For the co-ordinator, the issue is about ways of supporting colleagues to facilitate differentiation in their subject area.

Before focusing on supporting a colleague, you will need to work within your own classroom. Monitor how at least two children in a small group cope with a worksheet/task you have given them for your subject area. This may be a worksheet that you have designed yourself, or it may be a commercially produced one. Or you may choose a practically based task.

- How long do they spend on the task? Is this what you would expect?
- Are they having any problems, or is the work apparently very easy for them? What kinds of 'mistakes', if any, are they making?
- What can you deduce about 'task match' from the ease or difficulty of their working?
- Were there differences between the two children and, if so, how have you accommodated them?
- How far are Andrew Pollard's comments, above, about social task match, applicable?

This evidence could be the basis of an in-service discussion with colleagues regarding matching tasks in your subject area. It also gives you an indication of the range of issues to be addressed when supporting someone else. As a co-ordinator, your support of colleagues is likely to be focused on a specific subject. You will be looking at the range of teaching strategies employed by your colleagues and the tasks offered to pupils. We will focus on working in a colleague's class in Chapter 9, but it is appropriate to discuss this here in relation to the issue of differentiation. You will probably be observing, rather than working alongside your colleague, when focusing on differentiation. As part of this, you will need to talk to the pupils in the class about the tasks given. You will need to keep some notes as you observe for subsequent discussion and review after the period of observation. It is essential to discuss with your colleague the specific focus of any observation that you undertake; some teachers feel the lack of resources precludes particular teaching strategies. With your emphasis on a subject, you will look at employing an appropriate range of pupil-learning strategies, even if there are a limited range of resources. Other aspects of the classroom that you might look at are: the physical organisation of the classroom, including the use of space, display etc; the number of activities planned and the areas of the curriculum addressed; pace and use of time; and the availability of support and behaviour of pupils.

Continuity

Before moving on to look at progression, it is important to be aware of the continuity which is needed to ensure progression. Progression requires that individual teachers plan for a coherent and progressive experience of a subject for the pupils in their class. Different teachers and different schools which have responsibility for the same pupils over a period of time need to work together to ensure a continuity of experience for their pupils.

In determining how continuity can best be achieved, there are a number of different items that need to be considered: the schemes of work for a subject, assessment and recording policies, resource and materials, classroom organisation, and the teaching and learning styles for a subject. The co-ordinator's role is to be aware of the differences that will exist between different teachers and different schools and to consider how these might affect the continuity of experience for pupils. They must also ensure that, through discussion and the sharing of approaches, arrangements are made to establish the essential components of the provision of experience of a subject for all pupils. This may require the co-ordinator to liaise with feeder institutions in order to enable this continuity to be established.

Progression

Curricular progression must take account not only of curriculum 'coverage', but also of learning. The children's individual records of achievement are used, together with specific pieces of work, by each teacher to record learning across the curriculum. Collectively, the folders for each class form the basis of discussion with the next teacher.

Miller (1989) suggests that progression can be divided into progression of concepts, contexts and processes, as follows:

- conceptual progression is concerned with the way in which children's capacity to use general organising principles, or concepts, develops;

- contextual progression is concerned with matching the complexity-of-learning contexts to children's conceptual understanding;
- process progression is concerned with progression into more complex processes of thinking, interaction and enquiry.

Does this seem an adequate analysis to you? Could you improve it? How?

In order to base school-level planning on children's learning, careful record-keeping must be developed. Some schools are finding ways of involving the children themselves in the process of keeping records of their learning; this includes evidence of children's work. Both child and teacher can then interpret the children's learning. These records are a useful tool for forward planning for each child, because they contain not simply the teacher's assumption of what has been learned, but also evidence of learning, together with an interpretation from both child and teacher.

> Select an idea for developing curricular progression in your curriculum area, for example, taking a concept to be developed during the years that a child is in your school. This could be the basis of a staff meeting used to plan out the tasks/activities that would facilitate progression. An important aspect here will be the continuity of experience that a child has throughout the school. This is not an area fully addressed in this course, but must be considered alongside progression. Try it out, and record notes for later use. The detail of the National Curriculum policies can mean that record-keeping of learning, although onerous, is potentially very detailed; but it is planning that truly achieves and builds on progression and needs to be detailed. How well does your school stand up to scrutiny of its curricular progression?
>
> - Focus on an aspect of your curriculum area, in which curricular progression in your own school is good, and say why. You could use Miller's distinctions between conceptual, contextual and process progression. Be specific about the evidence which supports your claim.
> - Identify those aspects of your curriculum area in which progression is weak. What needs to be done? How can you find evidence of learning as well as coverage? What could be your contribution?

Whole-school and class-level planning: a comparison

Now we move to looking more closely at the levels of planning and the processes and issues associated with each level. Planning at whole-school level enables you to focus on the continuity and progression of the children's experiences in school as they move through the classes. You need also to check progress within a class, as well as helping to ensure that a balance of learning is planned across the curriculum from year to year. So planning at school level enables us to do some things which we cannot achieve at the class or micro level.

- Drawing on the work and thinking that you have done on this chapter of the book, brainstorm all the strengths of whole-school planning, at its ideal and best. What can it enable you to do?
- Next, brainstorm all of the things which it cannot do, and which you see as being the weaknesses of whole-school planning.
- Highlight the strengths and weaknesses of whole-school planning for your curriculum area.

A teacher wrote the following for this activity:

Strengths of whole-school planning
1. Everyone is involved and is aware of shared aims.
2. It gives support to all staff and is particularly helpful to inexperienced teachers.
3. Through planning together all have a chance to contribute, and a 'whole' school picture evolves.
4. A consensus is reached, aims are shared, and all work towards them.
5. Staff are made aware of how other parts of the school work, and can see whole-school progression and their part in it.
6. It should enable a school to achieve progression and continuity in the curriculum.
7. It allows staff to learn from each other.
8. Through discussion and listening to each other, staff are able to clarify their thinking.
9. Staff, for their own personal development, should not stick with one stage, and therefore knowledge of curricular development at all stages is essential.

Weaknesses of whole-school planning
1. It could, if not flexible, eliminate the opportunity for choice on the part of individuals.
2. It needs careful handling and an understanding of group dynamics. The management needs to understand and appreciate individual differences in staff and their strengths and weaknesses.
3. It cannot make a 'bad' teacher into a 'good' teacher, but then no planning can.
4. Lack of flexibility on the part of management could lead to unsatisfactory whole-school planning.

Perhaps your analysis was similar. In identifying strengths, this teacher focused on structural and interpersonal aspects (her statements numbered 1, 2, 7 and 8), as well as the curricular and learning content (her statements numbered 3, 4, 5, 6 and 9). In looking for weaknesses in whole-school planning, however, she focused purely on the structural and interpersonal aspects. To these we would add curricular and learning weaknesses: that whole-school planning cannot provide in any detail for individuals or groups on a day-to-day level in the classroom; it cannot be responsive to learning in a way that micro-level planning might be. Both are necessary if you are 'educating the child'.

Summary

In this chapter you have thought about and analysed your own and your school's practice from five perspectives:

1. how far specific curriculum documents, policy or advice guide the content and approaches of your curricular planning;
2. subject-based or thematic planning and its relationship to your subject;
3. subject specialism and how this matches with your views on integrated/subject-specific teaching and learning;
4. differentiation;
5. progression.

We will now go on to look at evaluation and the planning of teaching and learning.

Suggestions for the reader

1. Think carefully about the balance between the subject and project teaching which you choose in your own practice, and examine the reasons which underlie your choice.

2. When you have considered your practice as a whole, focus on the subject(s) which you are the co-ordinator for. How far do you integrate this curriculum area? Write down which aspects, if any, you integrate, and the reasons why you do so. Then make a list of any aspects which you teach as a separate subject, and your reasons for this.

3. Try the activity, using the statements for working in an integrated way and those for working within a subject, with your colleagues. You may feel that it is more appropriate to focus the sorting and associated discussion on your subject.

4. Jot down your ideas on curricular integration/curricular specialists in your notebook, indicating what balance you think is appropriate to your school.

5. In the light of your reading and your current working context, draw up a list of the advantages and disadvantages for specialist teaching by the co-ordinator.

6. Review your own plans from the viewpoint of differentiating the curriculum. Look at your plans for the work in your classroom this week. Focus on your co-ordination subject.

   • How have you differentiated the formal curriculum for different children or groups?
   • How would you convey what you have done to differentiate the curriculum to your colleagues?
   • How useful are the categories of differentiation given here? Are there any missing?

7. Observe two children as part of a small group working on a task/activity given for your subject area. Think about the issues raised by Andrew Pollard's comments earlier in the chapter to assist with focusing your observation. If you can talk to the children about the activity afterwards, find out their perceptions of the activity and whether they match yours.

8. Carry out the same activity with a colleague and discuss your observations afterwards.

6
Evaluation

Introduction

In this chapter, you will be evaluating your planning for individuals, groups and your class, as well as your role as planner in your whole school. You will be considering your aims for each of these levels, identifying the kind of evidence that you will need in order to evaluate your progress in respect of these aims, and making decisions about how to collect data. Evidence about children's learning will play a major role in your evaluation, since without this evidence you cannot evaluate planning.

Shipman (1979) makes the following three assumptions about evaluation:

1. it is not an optional extra, but is integral to an effective curriculum;
2. it should involve judgement;
3. it should incorporate a variety of responses.

These can be applied to any activity that you undertake as a co-ordinator, and should be part of your planning process. Remember the variety of responses for evaluation: verbal, written, or like a questionnaire in format. Figure 38 on page 141 shows ways in which to ask participants to comment on talks and workshops.

First, however, it is worth making a few distinctions and working through some principles of evaluation.

Some distinctions: assessment, evaluation and review

Assessment, evaluation and review are sometimes confused with one another, although they are, in fact, fairly distinct concepts (which at times overlap). For the purpose of this module, we suggest the following definitions:

- Assessment is concerned with the process of gathering information (by teachers, pupils and others) about learning, in order to determine achievement; this information may form part of the data on which an evaluation draws.
- Evaluation, on the other hand, is concerned with appraising many aspects of teaching and learning to see if the intended aims have been realised – it may also include a re-examination of aims. The kind of evaluation that we are concerned with in this module involves considering learning outcomes against aims by using certain indicators, or criteria, to tell us to what extent the aims have been met. This is criterion-referenced evaluation.

A distinction is sometimes made between formative and summative evaluation. Formative evaluation provides regular feedback in order to improve teaching and learning on a day-to-day basis; summative evaluation occurs at the end of a period of time and forms the basis on which judgments can be made regarding how far the objectives have been met at that time. In fact, summative evaluation also plays a formative role, since it informs the next cycle of planning and learning.

Review plays two roles in the evaluation cycle. Firstly, it involves reflecting on the period to be evaluated in order to begin the process of evaluating the extent to which the criteria were met. It forms the analytical part of the cycle and it involves reconsidering whether the assumptions, aims, priorities and approach should be changed on the basis of evaluation evidence. Evaluation and review can be described in the cycle shown in Figure 18.

It is important to be clear about who your audience is – in other words, who the evaluation is for. In the case of evaluating the planning of learning for individual children, for groups and for your whole class, your

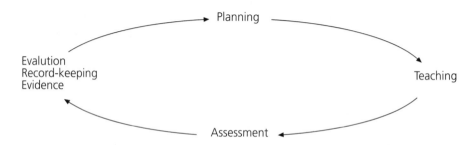

FIGURE 18 *The cycle of planning, teaching, assessing, reviewing and evaluation. The planning cycle is a continuous one in which each element cannot be seen as an isolated aspect, since they are all linked.*

main 'audience' will be yourself, whereas in evaluating the school-level planning of learning, the audience may be the whole body of staff, parents, and possibly the governors or school board. The evaluation outcomes will remain the same, though the reports may differ.

Evaluation criteria and evidence

A criterion is a standard by which you can evaluate your original aim. You will often be using not just one criterion, but a set of criteria. You have considered planning criteria and have collected evidence for these criteria in order to help you evaluate the realisation of your aims and plans. Evidence about the criteria will help you to evaluate your plans for them.

As you work through evaluation at each level, you will be returning to your own aims and identifying the appropriate criteria and evidence through which to make sense of what actually happened when the plans were translated into practice.

Methods of collecting evaluation evidence

The different techniques for collecting evidence represent varying degrees of subjectivity and objectivity. In addition to questionnaires, documentary evidence, discussion, interview, observations, and evidence from pupils, the pupils themselves can be involved by means of forms of self-evaluation of the activities they have undertaken.

Questionnaires

These can involve open-ended questions, such as 'What have you learned today?' 'What helped the learning?' 'How did this happen?' 'Was there anything which you would have liked to spend more time/less time on?' With very young children, this kind of questionnaire, rather than being written, might form the basis of a discussion with each child on a regular basis.

Questionnaires can also involve structured questions, requiring ticked or graded answers which then produce a response sheet, which is easy to analyse. However, this gives children no opportunity to provide a personal response and in this way runs against the principles of the 'constructivist' approach to learners which we have been building up. The constructivist approach takes serious account of the sense that children make of learning situations, rather than imposing our own meanings on them. In our view, therefore, a structured questionnaire approach is inappropriate.

Lastly, questionnaires can involve sentence-completion tasks, such as
'I have learned ...' or 'I thought this activity was ... (because ...)'.
Again, with young children, this kind of question could be put in the
form of painting, drawing, modelling or discussion, rather than writing.
If the answer is to be a written one, the amount of time made available
and the amount of space on the paper will, of course, affect the response,
just as an oral response, for example, will be constrained by the time
allowed as well as other circumstances of the evaluation (such as when
and where the discussion is taking place).

Other documentary evidence

All evaluation involves referring back to aims. This will include looking
back at your original plans, together with school policy documents and
National, or LEA, Curriculum guidelines. Documentary evaluation evidence will include any records of learning kept by yourself, the children
and any other partners in planning and learning, such as parents. The
records will include learning outcomes, such as children's writing, a record
of reading or a miscue analysis, and models, paintings, and so on – as well
as those records specially created by the children during reviewing.

FIGURE 19 *The collection of students' work*

*A way of using pupils' work more fully as a resource involves the co-ordinator extending
the range of work undertaken. A variety of rationales are given below for the collection
of students' work.*

KS1 Assessment Order 1993
Regulation 6
(3) On request by the verifying authority the head teacher shall provide them with
the results of teacher assessments and standard task assessments of such
number or proportion of pupils and in such subjects or attainment targets of
subjects as they may require, together with the supporting material referred to in
paragraph (4), to enable the verifying authority to verify the assessments.
(4) The supporting material consists of the records and other evidence of a pupil's
achievements relied on by a teacher in making a teacher assessment, the pupil's
written response to the standard tasks and such further material as the authority
may reasonably require.

Circular 11/93
Section V 13
Head teachers will want to ensure that there is a coherent school policy in place to:
● gather and record evidence of pupils' attainments in relation to the attainment
  targets.
Head teachers will need to see to it that teachers working at key stage 1 have taken
steps to draw on evidence of attainment yielded by:
● observations of practical work in the classroom
● written work completed in class.

Section VI 17
The head teacher and governing body have specific duties:
● to meet reasonable requests from the auditors for samples of pupils' written work undertaken as part of the standard tasks and of samples of pupils' work underpinning teachers' own assessments.
It will not be necessary for this purpose for schools to keep evidence of the attainments of every pupil in every attainment target. The portfolios of work which schools typically build up of pupils' work should now be fully sufficient. The key thing will be to have representative samples of work which, in the school's judgment, illustrate the standards expected in each of the core subjects at each of the levels of attainment.

Circular 17/89
The Education (School Records) Regulations 1989
para. 15
. . . Two distinct but related purposes [of records] need to be borne particularly in mind:
i. the need to be able to present to other teachers and the parents concerned throughout any key stage, basic data on how any given pupil is progressing within any given attainment target in terms of the National Curriculum attainment levels 1–10, and whether or not the assessments have been validated under statutory assessment procedures. . . .
ii. the need for teachers to be able to bring forward *evidence* to support their assessment of pupils' levels of attainment, in particular for the end of key stage assessments.

Circulars, whilst reiterating the need for 'evidence', offer little guidance of what this constitutes. However SEAC and NCC (now amalgamated as Schools Curriculum and Assessment Authority (SCAA)) publications offer clearer guidance.

(SEAC 1991) [Case Studies from Schools]

pages 8–11 Account 3

Recording ephemeral evidence:
Some of the most important *evidence* of pupils' attainment arises as pupils are discussing their work with their teacher or when they are working practically or conducting an investigation.

pages 34–36

Building up a folder of evidence:
In building up folders, there is a need to agree criteria for selecting, reviewing and replacing pupils' work and other evidence.

Although all SoA need to be addressed, it is neither possible nor desirable to collect evidence for every pupil against every SoA.

Source: Essex Development and Advisory Service (EDAS)'s Assessment, Recording and Reporting of Achievement Team (1994).

FIGURE 20 *Positive reasons for keeping evidence*

What is evidence?

It can be anything which helps build up a picture of pupils' achievements. For example:

- teachers' planning notes;
- teachers' and pupils' records;
- notes of observations;
- notes of discussions;
- the pupils' work;
- tape recordings/videos;
- photographs etc;
- artefacts.

Collecting evidence does not involve:

- collecting all the work every pupil has ever done;
- making notes of every interaction between you and a pupil or between the pupil and his/her peers.

and it is not something merely collected at the end of the key stage.

There are two positive reasons for keeping evidence:

1. To support the child:

To encourage the pupil to reflect on his or her own achievements and to be involved in identifying his or her future learning needs.
To inform and facilitate discussions about a pupil's achievements with parents and others who have a need to know.

'Two key principles underpin the gathering and recording of evidence:

- it is an integral part of the plans for learning; teachers must provide children with the opportunity to reflect on what they have done. Material which is kept, collected and selected by the child and the teacher will help the child to review the success and progress of their learning;
- it should lead to a response; gathering and recording evidence is not an end in itself but a means of informing the next stage of learning for the child.'
  (English Non-Statutory Guidance Page D1)

2. To support the school:

To help standardise assessments within and across schools.
To support teacher assessment at the end of the key stage.

Many schools have begun the process of building up a whole-school collection of evidence of children's responses to classroom activities.

This process offers an opportunity for all staff to engage in discussion about the assessment of those responses and to reach agreement about any attainment.

Interesting responses from children in the school are discussed, annotated and, when agreement is reached, are placed in the school '**R**ecord **O**f **L**earning **O**utcomes' (ROLO).

The ROLO serves a number of purposes:

- the process of building it up helps reassure all members of staff that their judgements are in line with those of their colleagues;
- new members of staff (and visitors to the school) are able to refer to it to gain understanding of the school's assessment standards;
- the selected learning outcomes can help demonstrate to those who need to know (e.g. new members of staff, parents, governors, auditors, inspectors) the kind of responses which were expected from a child before that child's individual records were marked to indicate attainment.

Source: Essex Development and Advisory Service (EDAS)'s Assessment, Recording and Reporting of Achievement Team (1994).

FIGURE 21 *Purposes of individual and school portfolios*

'School portfolios will provide sample evidence for moderation purposes.' 'The school portfolio of recent work is the most efficient and manageable way for many schools to demonstrate the judgements they are making. This should illustrate all aspects of the core curriculum and the range of levels attained by pupils in the school. The school portfolio should include the teachers' notes of ephemeral evidence as well as the children's written work. It should be annotated to give contextual background and to indicate the levels of attainment as well as the justifications for those judgements (KSI DRAFT SAF 1993)

'The individual portfolio of assessment evidence for each child serves a different purpose from the school portfolio. Its function is to provide motivation for the child, who can see progress being made, and is very useful as a basis for discussing progress with the parent. Only in very exceptional circumstances will it be needed for moderation.' (KSI DRAFT SAF 1993) An individual portfolio can help encourage a child to evaluate his/her own progress, through reflection on and discussion about samples of work selected for inclusion. 'The quality of pupils' learning is to be judged in terms of: learning skills, including ... evaluating work done.' (FRAMEWORK FOR THE INSPECTION OF SCHOOLS, p18)

Note: As a result of work undertaken by EDAS's Assessment, Recording and Reporting of Achievement (ARRA) Team, a number of schools in Essex became involved in a pilot for producing a ROLO (a school's record of learning outcomes).
Source: EDAS's ARRA Team.

FIGURE 22 *A school's record of learning outcomes (ROLO)*

A ROLO is a collection of children's responses to the school curriculum which may be exemplified by pieces of their work or other records of their learning, including plans and teacher notes of responses.

Any responses need contextualising if the ROLO is to be used by a range of professionals.

A ROLO is, in the first instance, a means by which schools can identify and agree points of progress in the National Curriculum and may initially choose to address core subjects. In this instance, the ROLO needs also to be an easily accessible reference to the levels in the National Curriculum.

In the second and further instances, the ROLO is used as an exemplification of the range and variety of the school curriculum for use with fellow teachers, children, new members of staff, parents, governors, inspectors etc.

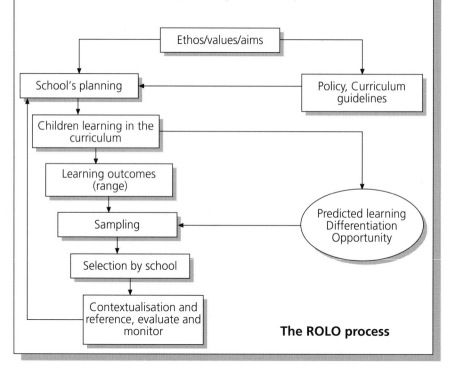

Source: Essex Development and Advisory Service (EDAS)'s Assessment, Recording and Reporting of Achievement Team (1994).

FIGURE 23 *Why develop a ROLO?*

A ROLO provides:

- a manageable and practical approach to the use of evidence in school;
- a window on the school curriculum;
- a useful monitoring and evaluation process;
- an immediate and accessible means of recognising and valuing teaching and learning in the school;

- a process which raises standards;
- a manifestation of school aims, ethos and policy.

Checklist for developing a ROLO in school
A ROLO is a process which documents the learning outcomes of a school – not of individuals. It is important, when coming to decisions about what to sample and select, that choices are made to reflect the range and the diversity within the school curriculum rather than representing on an individual, class or year-group basis.

Sampling
When sampling outcomes to reflect progress in the National Curriculum across the school, you may find it useful to choose examples which do not necessarily sit happily in a level. Annotation on discussion about why it does not, for instance, showing particular evidence in the next level up, or down, can be helpful to a colleague at a future point.

If your policy is that assessment should take place in the learning context, then you should not set up teaching/learning situations specially for the purposes of the ROLO. Sampling should become a more natural process after a while, when work is sampled to reflect the school curriculum as it unfolds over time. Teachers may save up significant samples to discuss at a ROLO meeting.

Selection
Selection of outcomes needs to be made at a whole-school level. Initially meetings may involve the whole staff, particularly where work is referenced to National Curriculum levels. It may become the responsibility of the post holder for quality assurance.

ROLO meetings need to be a regular occurrence. A timetable for focus meetings needs to be drawn up to reflect the school's long-term planning cycles.

Annotation
Decisions need to be made early on about how learning outcomes are to be annotated and contextualised. The school may choose to use a particular format for this purpose.

Contextualisation should convey curriculum context in relation to subject focus (medium-term planning), learning focus (short-term planning) and the National Curriculum.

The contextualisation also needs to convey relevant detail not apparent through the outcome evidence itself. This may include detail about learning styles, prior experience or related learning, predicted outcome etc.

It is important to make reference to National Exemplar material if discussing the relation of outcomes to National Curriculum levels.

Results of whole-staff agreement made with reference to, for example, the National Curriculum, need to be attached to or kept with the learning outcome.

Where a ROLO is being developed to record outcomes beyond the core NC subjects, decisions need to be made about how progress is to be identified and referenced.

You will need to bear in mind potential users and uses. These will include:

- children;
- existing colleagues;
- new colleagues;
- existing/potential parents;
- governors;

- other visitors and professionals;
- National Curriculum Audit;
- Ofsted inspection;
- ARRA Accreditation;
- transfer liaison meetings.

Source: Essex Development and Advisory Service (EDAS)'s Assessment, Recording and Reporting of Achievement Team (1994).

Pitsea County Infant School, Essex, was one of the first schools in the authority to take part in piloting this approach. Its mathematics co-ordinator had been given information about the ROLO on a course. She took this back to the head and the rest of the staff who expressed interest in being part of the pilot stage. Of key importance here was the support for the initiative from the head and staff. As a result of this, the school began the process with mathematics, also leading into other curriculum areas.

The purpose had to be clear before attempting to collect any samples of work even though, because of the school's perception of assessment, the need for such a document had already been recognised. From the outset, this was clearly going to be an ongoing document which need to be updated.

The co-ordinator collected samples from all staff and initially sorted them into attainment targets. For a specific subject this was useful, as it highlighted the balance within the subject as a whole. Then each of the samples of work was discussed by the staff. At this stage a number of principles were established. Firstly, that the work would be anonymous and would not have children's ages on samples. A variety of forms of evidence were established as valid, for example photographs and transcripts. There was a need to explain the context for pieces of work. Once the level had been agreed, then everyone on the staff would sign in order to signal their agreement. This would include working towards a level, not just achieving a level.

After several lengthy staff meetings in which these principles were established, the samples of work became a regular agenda item. The co-ordinator oversees that process during the staff meeting, and is responsible for asking for samples of work during any gaps. More generally, the co-ordinator encourages staff to contribute samples at any time, and ensures that the document is kept up to date and in the staff room for the easy access of all staff.

The benefits that the school feels it has obtained from the process are as follows:

- it is useful for planning;
- it is useful as a standard measure;
- it helps teachers new to the school;
- it helps teachers changing class internally;
- it shows parents and governors the progression and continuity of work within the school;
- it is a celebration of children's work;
- it encourages teachers to talk together and share, particularly for mathematics AT 1;
- it ensures a balanced view of mathematics;
- the whole staff has looked more closely at practice and this has provided a focus for staff thinking;
- it has highlighted a school standard rather than that of the individual child.

The experience outlined by the mathematics co-ordinator at Pitsea County Infant School demonstrates a specific role in co-ordinating evidence of children's work. Either discuss how you might undertake such a task in your school or discuss this with other co-ordinators within your school or in other schools in order to compare your experiences.

Discussion

Large group discussions tend to produce either very positive or very negative comments, and can deny the majority of the participants the chance to speak in depth, as well as increasing the likelihood of the focus being lost. A more productive way of organising discussions can be to ask children to work in pairs or trios and list and record, for example, six good things and six bad things about the learning experience. They can then compare these with another pair and report on them to the whole group. The composite list of good and bad points is built up on a large sheet of paper, or on the board, by the teacher during this report, and the children can then vote on the order that the components should be in.

Another idea for older children is to identify review criteria and to give groups a fixed time to discuss and record views on each, which are then fed back into the whole class. Each child's view should be recorded.

A further idea for varying whole-group discussions is to take the points raised by children in an open-ended questionnaire, or in a group brainstorming session, and to use these for discussion. The points can be organised into a structured questionnaire first, giving every child a way of indicating the extent to which he or she agrees with each point. This means that the points which are discussed are those on which there are differences of opinion. A way of encouraging children to reflect on what other members of a large group are saying is to introduce a rule that everything said must follow on from what somebody else has said.

Children are thus encouraged to listen and to make connections between their own experience and that of others.

Interviewing

The same principle as outlined for questionnaires applies to interviews: as well as being offered a structure, children should be offered opportunities to say what they feel in an open-ended way. This means prioritising listening, and remembering that 'one generally gleans more information by talking with rather than talking to' (Harris and Bell, 1990).

Interviews can be structured, partially structured or unstructured. Partially structured interviews are a useful evaluation technique. This kind of interview needs to be planned carefully beforehand. Planning is likely to involve:

- deciding which issues you want to raise;
- deciding how to record the information;
- framing questions and follow-up questions;
- re-writing any questions which seem ambiguous, hard to answer, or which do not appear to provide what you want to know.

Interviews that are completely unstructured, on the other hand, can also yield information that may not emerge through other methods, but they need to be carefully planned, have a definite purpose, and be carried out by a person who has practice and skill in interviewing.

Group interviews can be helpful, in that ideas can sometimes be sparked off more easily, although this can also distort what individuals actually think or feel, and the group dynamic which is set up can exclude some children.

We already know that encouraging children to reflect over what they have learned and what could be improved can help them to progress. For this to have the greatest effect, however, we need to give thought to how to help children to be critical and focused in their thinking.

The ways in which individuals make sense of, and interpret, meaning are personal. Therefore, when we interview children, we find that their answers do not always reflect what we want or expect. Children's responses often tell us a lot about what they are interested in, what they found difficult or couldn't understand and do, etc; you may have found this, too, during your own interview. We don't find the information that we want because the children are unused to analysing their own learning, and because our method of collecting the data requires refinement.

Observation

Using audio or video recordings of specific activities can give you evaluation information, although this is very time-consuming. Deliberately and closely observing children at work can give you the same kind of feedback but without the advantage of replay. This can involve watching as an 'official audience', for example, during a class assembly, or it can mean 'eavesdropping' on children at work.

The focus of your observation will, of course, be the evaluation criteria. It can sometimes be helpful to structure observations around your focus. Structured observations can often be 'closed': for example, a 'closed' observation schedule could be used with a drama rehearsal group, and might include views concerning the talk and leadership in the group or the quality of learning and understanding in the history curriculum.

Recording evaluation information from discussions, interviews and observations

Perhaps the most obvious way of recording information is by taking notes. Since most people have a tendency to hear, observe and record what pleases them, having a written record can offer a way of exposing and exploring bias – particularly if the evaluation notes are triangulated, or made by three or more people.

Pre-prepared check lists can also be used during interviews and discussions as a reminder and prompt to you, as the evaluator. They can be especially useful in recording initial responses and comments. An example of a check list might be:

- What do you enjoy, and why, in this project?
- What do you choose to record and why?
- What do you think history is?
- What kinds of learning do you enjoy?

What else would you want to add to this check list? Or how might you adopt this for an activity focusing on your subject?

Evaluating individual children

Evaluating the extent to which your plans have enabled each child to achieve depth of learning in each part of the curriculum is an onerous task because you need to collect evidence from individual children, and this can take time. Some teachers evaluate their planning for individual children at specific points during the year, such as at each half-term, or each term. Through evaluating your plans for individual children at regular intervals, you may find that you need to reconsider the way in which you approach your scheme of work and the basis on which you plan differential work, both here and on a day-to-day basis.

So far, you have been focusing on the evaluation of learning and have been using this to review your planning. But you may also need to challenge and reconsider the assumptions on which the plans are made from time to time.

> Look back over the aims, assumptions, priorities and approach of the plans for the same two children that you chose for the monitoring activity in the previous chapter, and reconsider them.
>
> - How appropriate were the aims, assumptions, priorities and approach of the plans from the point of view of the two children and from that of the curriculum? If the children were involved in creating these aims, you will need to involve them in the review. You might want to ask the children to think back to their planning, and to try to remember why they had these aims right at the start, what they thought was important, and why they wanted to work in the ways that they did.
> - Is there anything that you or the children would now want to change, or that has already been changed, and why?

Evaluating groups

The way in which you evaluate groups will depend on your approach to, and planning for, group formation.

In some schools, children are grouped according to certain criteria, for example, friendship groups, 'ability', mixed ability, or gender. Groupings are used differently by individual teachers; some hold for the whole curriculum, whereas others regroup children for different subjects. More rigid grouping of children enables their teachers to keep track of what is planned and learned by the children more easily than in those classrooms where the groupings are more fluid – but this means that learning opportunities are less responsive to individual needs. In classrooms in which groupings are more fluid, the planning of learning opportunities may be more flexible; record-keeping, of course, also needs to be more individualised. The extent to which your own approach to grouping offers children equal opportunities in learning and matches their learning needs – including issues such as motivation, interest and personal connections – should be the focus of evaluation at times.

Evaluating at class level

Of the many aspects of class-level planning, we want you to focus here on planning the learning environment.

The learning environment

We will start off by thinking about the learning environment (which includes the ethos of the classroom, hidden curricular issues, classroom organisation and management).

Evaluation at the level of classroom organisation, management and methods can be very revealing. Research has been carried out by a number of different practitioners into what happens when class-level plans are translated into practice, on a day-to-day level, with infant children. Barbara Tizard and colleagues (1988), whose work we referred to in Chapter 3, revealed in their study that the children spent up to 43 per cent of the total day involved in non-work activities, and that, of their working time, 64 per cent was spent on 'basic' activities: 17 per cent on mathematics, 20 per cent on writing and 27 per cent on other language activities such as reading, discussion and story time.

A percentage distribution is now reflected to some extent in the revised 1994 National Curriculum at key stage one. How much of the planned organisation, management and ethos of your subject area revealed 'lost' time in your evaluation?

Record-keeping

This subsection focuses on record-keeping for your subject area and your role as co-ordinator in that process.

> Look at your own system of conveying information to other people about children's learning in your subject area.
>
> - What do you currently do?
> - Choose the audience for your evaluation.
> - Drawing on ideas from this section of the chapter, decide on the criteria and the evidence that you will use. You might like to consider criteria which relate to children and parents, as well as to teachers.
> - Choose your methods of evaluation and triangulation.
> - Carry out your evaluation and jot down its outcomes. What are the implications for your own practice and for colleagues' practice?

Evaluation of the effectiveness of your record-keeping may lead you to re-establish the kinds of information which you, parents, children and other teachers require. As teachers, we often record information which is necessary in terms of the curricular framework, but which does not necessarily take account of either:

- what parents and children feel should be recorded;
- the sense that parents and children make of it.

FIGURE 24 *Foci for observation*

Observation schedule

Class	Time observed	Date	Subject observed

Attainment targets/programme of study addressed

Cross-curricular links

Pupils
Attitude
Response
Attainment
Behaviour
Progress

Teaching strategies employed
Whole class
Group
Individual
Discussion
Worksheets/scheme material
Practical task/use of equipment

Classroom
Display
Resources
Organisation

Equal opportunities schedule

Pupils
Number of girls and boys in the class
Groupings for lesson/period observed
Are tasks given to girls different from those given to boys?

Teaching
Teacher/pupil interaction with girls
Teacher/pupil interaction with boys

Classroom
Does the display reflect the range of ability of the class?
Does the display reflect differing interests?
Does the display reflect a balance of male/female characters, interests and approaches?

Resources
Is there a balance of resources reflecting male/female issues?
Have the resources been checked for bias?
Are stereotypes explored directly, if appropriate?

Part of your role as a curriculum co-ordinator is to monitor the implementation of the National Curriculum and the school's policy of practice. So far we have concentrated mainly on observation in your class. In order to make observations beyond your own class, you may wish to use one of the observation schedules in Figure 24. These are only guides, and do not represent an exhaustive list of aspects for observation. As a whole-staff group, you may wish to use these suggested schedules as the basis for developing your own.

When you have tried out these observation schedules in your own class, you can then negotiate to try them in a colleague's class. You may also feel confident enough to let a colleague use them for the basis of observation in your class (in itself a learning opportunity: how do you think this may feed into your observation of colleagues in their classrooms?). Since colleagues will be co-ordinating another subject area, they may well carry out differing observations in your classroom though focusing on their subject.

You may wish to make notes on the appropriateness of the focus of the schedules. If your school is considering how observations can be carried out by co-ordinators, then you may wish to use the suggested schedules as the basis of discussion. You will need to consider the following: what would you change? Would all the schedules be the same? Do you need specific foci for particular subjects? How will this information be used? What form of feedback will be given to those observed? Consider how questions are phased and whether everything you would want to address is covered. Add your own ideas.

You should discuss the record made after the observation. It is important to provide, or to be provided with, feedback on the process, as well as any specific outcomes. As mentioned before, there needs to be agreement on the form and scale of the feedback that might be expected by those observed.

As part of this process, you may find it useful to refer to any material contained in school about the appraisal (review in Scotland) and inspection process. The appraisal cycle will look at your role as a co-ordinator. The inspection-process material details the criteria for efficiency that will be used in judging your school. Efficient use of staff time and resources come under criteria for efficiency.

Evaluating at the whole-school level

A full school-level evaluation of planning should involve everyone who takes part in the planning process. Of course, this level and scale of evaluation involves starting by viewing evaluation as an essential part of managing the school. A whole-school evaluation should, like other levels of evaluation, be clear about its audience. It is not uncommon for reports to be produced for the audiences of whole-school evaluations, and, because this is an enormous area, we are going to focus here on evaluating your contribution to one aspect of school-level planning, over the past school year.

Look back over your school's curriculum and learning policies or, if there is one, the school-development plan, and choose aspect of curriculum planning at whole-school level in which you have been involved this year. You might choose your curriculum area, if that is appropriate.

- Who is the audience for this evaluation? What were your curricular and learning aims? What will be the criteria by which you can judge your success in achieving these aims as a planner, and what evidence do you need?
- What methods of evaluation will you choose?
- Review the whole-school planning of the curricular area in which you have been involved. Then, by considering what your chosen indicators tell you about your success as a planner in achieving your aims, evaluate and reconsider how this evaluation will influence your aims, priorities and approach. How will your planning need to change in the light of the evaluation? How will you communicate the results of your evaluation, and to whom? Report on both your evaluation and review in your notebook.

Your aims for whole-school planning may have included some very specific ones, such as 'developing a handwriting policy' in order to improve the pupils' handwriting. Underlying many of your aims at the whole-school level and your chosen area of the curriculum are the general principles of planning for continuity and progression, so your evaluation should be giving you feedback about these. A question that you should be asking yourself as a member of a whole-staff team is: how are the continuity policies, in and between schools, made explicit to parents and to children?

Evaluation information on your own role in whole-school planning may, or may not, be for whole-staff 'consumption', depending on the circumstances of the review.

Staying with the planning for the same curriculum area, identify your aims in terms of your own role as co-ordinator in this whole-school planning process, then:

- Decide on your criteria, evidence and audience for evaluation.
- Decide on a method, or methods, for collecting the evaluation data on your role and then carry it out.
- Note the key issues/areas and report back on them.

If you are able to, you should consider the following review questions in a pair. If you are working alone, write your response to each in your notebook.

- Were there any surprises?
- What are the areas that you will need to work on, and what will you need to do?

Summary

In this chapter you have reviewed the process of evaluating your own planning and the planning in which you are involved as a co-ordinator. You will have looked at different ways of collecting data as evidence for your evaluation. You will also be able to highlight areas of need for your planning as a co-ordinator. Since this is not a book primarily about evaluation, this chapter offers an introduction to the process and, if you are interested in this area, there are books written solely on this aspect which you might wish to read. It is important to make some judgments about how well activities have gone, and to understand the basis on which you might make those judgments. As a result you will be able to justify your decisions as a school/group/individual teacher and will be more secure in your judgments.

Suggestions for the reader

1. Select a learning activity in your curricular area to observe. As you observe, consider:

   - To what extent do you think the aims were achieved?
   - What surprised you, if anything?
   - What does this evaluation tell you about the planning?
   - How will this evaluation help you and/or the class teacher to plan forward?

2. Try this activity again, focusing on a child in another class. The observations could form the basis of work with a colleague.

3. Choose a group to evaluate in your own class, or, if you are not class based, a classroom to which you can gain access. You can decide the time frame of the evaluation; you might, for example, be evaluating today's plans, or your planning for a half-term.

   - What are the learning aims for this group? What are your criteria, and what evidence will you collect? Who will be the audience of the evaluation?
   - Which methods will you use, and why? You may find it helpful to use this activity as the basis of an in-service session with colleagues.

Try out your evaluation and reconsider your plans for the group in the light of your evaluation evidence. Were there any surprises? Any confirmations?

4. Choose an aspect of the learning environment or ethos in your classroom which you have planned to evaluate. Decide on your audience, criteria, evidence and methods, and then carry out the evaluation in the light of it, reviewing your planning at the same time.

5. Using the suggested observation schedules from this chapter, plan a staff meeting to discuss classroom observations by the co-ordinators in your school, and aim to produce an agreed school-wide schedule for those observations.

7
Policy documents

This chapter looks at policy documents and their content and formulation.

What is a policy document?

A policy document is a statement of the school's philosophy and beliefs regarding a particular area of the curriculum and the way in which it should be taught. It will attempt to be brief, and will obviously reflect the overall aims of the school. As the document is a result of developmental work carried out in the school, it will be updated in the light of future developments. The policy document should therefore have an introduction stating that: 'This policy document is a result of the development process to date, and we plan to ... at a future date.' (The dots indicate what type of future development work is planned to be carried out.) It will not include any subject content, since this will be in the scheme of work, but it will include examples of good work and practice.

For the curriculum area for which you are responsible, you will need to find the non-statutory guidance within the National Curriculum documents or other guidance documents provided for your education authority and county. These should contain references to policy documents or schools' policy statements, and to the areas that you will need to address, including:

- the purpose of your curricular area;
- the nature of your curricular area;
- the management of your curricular area, including planning procedures;
- how the National Curriculum will be taught;
- pupils' experiences of your curricular area;
- pupils' activities in your curricular area;
- pupils' records of their work in your curricular area;
- cross-curricular issues as they apply to your curricular area;

- the assessment of your curricular area: a) of individual pupils, b) of the teaching;
- recording pupils' progress in your curricular area;
- teachers' records;
- the evaluation of your curricular area;
- staffing and resources in your curricular area;
- the classroom management of your curricular area;
- health and safety;
- special needs;
- equal opportunities.

Here are some ideas of what a policy for a subject area might contain. References to:

- the school's ethos;
- the aims of subject teaching;
- the nature of subjects;
- cross-curricular issues, including: environmental issues, gender issues, other equal-opportunities issues (e.g. class), multicultural issues, gifted pupils, special educational needs, information technology;
- assessment, record-keeping and evaluation;
- classroom management and organisation, including: learning styles, teaching styles, the use of published scheme material, activities to be used, resources available, time allocation for subject, organisation of subject-teaching groups, role of the subject co-ordinator, professional development of staff (related to subject);
- Liaison with outside agencies, including: parents, schools from other phases (including play groups/nurseries), community (including local industry), learning support services, welfare services, child psychologists;
- further statements related to areas of the subject particular to your school.

All staff should play a part in the development of a subject policy document and it should be reviewed and updated regularly.

If looking at a specific curriculum area, for example geography, Rainey and Krause (1994) suggest the following:

The school geography policy document will vary a great deal from school to school, but it might contain:

- *a written statement showing the aims and objectives for geography;*
- *a key stage plan;*
- *a topic or unit plan which shows the place of geography within the whole curriculum;*

- *a description of how assessment in geography is linked to the school's overall assessment policy;*
- *a list of available resources;*
- *a plan showing details of resources to be obtained in the future;*
- *a list of places where members of staff can get help, such as local planning offices, and county records offices;*
- *a list of suitable places for class visits;*
- *details of an agreed school recording system for children's progress in geography;*
- *details of the local secondary schools' syllabus for geography in Y7;*
- *a timetable of appropriate TV broadcasts; and a list of suitable books, both fiction and non-fiction, with a geographical content;*
- *a schedule for the evaluation review of the policy. (Rainey and Krause, 1994.)*

> - Using the two lists of aspects to be included in a school policy, compile a list for your subject area. If you can, consult with colleagues and make the appropriate amendments to your list.
> - Find the school's policy for your curriculum area. Review the policy in the light of the list above, as well as in the light of your previous work, with particular reference to Chapter 4. When was it last reviewed? What updating does it require?

All staff concerned with teaching a particular subject area should be involved in contributing towards the policy statement, and in keeping it under review. It will form part of the overall curriculum policy of the school.

Three routes into the process of compiling a policy document might be as Figure 24 overleaf (a, b and c are alternative starting points).

> Read the following case study: 'Developing a policy for language: working with colleagues' by Jon Eyres, taken from the Open University's E628, *English in the primary curriculum: developing reading and writing*, Document 18. Jot down the issues raised here that are also common to your subject area.

Developing a policy for language: working with colleagues

Introduction

A former colleague of mine was recently invited to apply for the post of language co-ordinator in her new school. On enquiring what exactly the job would entail, she was told that she would be required to conduct a review of the language policy. As she recounted it, this would mean 'Two staff meetings: one reading, one writing!'

In this case study I shall outline how we began the task of formulating a completely new language policy for a large five-to-eleven primary school. I shall then look in more detail at how we approached the section

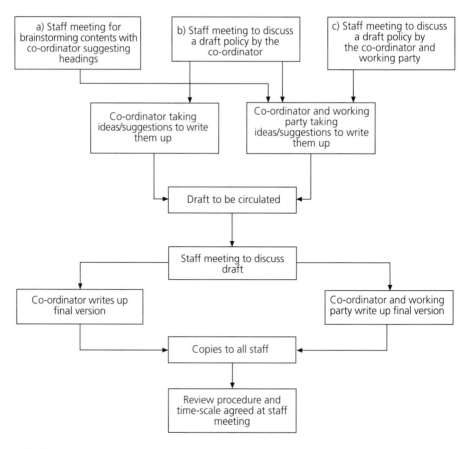

FIGURE 25 *Routes for compiling a policy document*

of the review concerned with writing. This was the area to which we devoted most time and also the one with which I was personally most closely involved. As I write, I have just put together what I hope will be the final draft of the policy. The work has involved all the staff and, at times, all the children in the school and has taken a total of five terms.

The context of the review
The school for which the policy has been written, Bar Hill Community Primary, serves Britain's first 'new village' – a completely self-contained development of almost exclusively private housing linked by the A604 trunk road to the city of Cambridge, some five miles away. In twenty years the school has grown from a single-class village school to its present size of thirteen classes and some 380 children, who come virtually exclusively from the village. Socially, then, the school's intake is about as homogeneous as it is possible to be in England in the 1990s.

Four years ago, a newly appointed head teacher began the task of changing the curriculum from one which was formal and traditional to one in which children would take a more active role in their own learning and motivation would come from tasks well chosen to suit the needs of individual children. Some major changes (e.g. the introduction of topic work) were brought about immediately, largely by diktat. Some brief statements on 'pervasive issues' (special needs, equal opportunities, IT, community and multicultural education) had been agreed, and more recently the staff had worked together to arrive at a 'view of the child'. The language review, however, was to be the first major review of a curriculum area under the new headship.

There was a need for a review. A variety of approaches to language teaching were in use. Some staff clearly regretted the passing of a formal ethos (and of these a few were later to put forward a determined resistance to change), while others (including a number who, like myself, had joined the school quite recently) had clear ideas about the new directions which they wanted language policy to take. A significant number of teachers, however, could not have been placed within either of these groups.

Although I would certainly not wish to argue that all teachers should be working in exactly the same way, it was in some cases causing problems when there were fundamental differences of outlook. So that children would be able to carry what they had learned in terms of skills and attitudes from one class to the next, and in order to avoid unfortunate comparisons between parallel classes, an agreed approach became necessary. There was a further reason for conducting a review. Many of the reforms carried out so far in the school, although in themselves both welcome and necessary, were either product-centred (e.g. children should make their own books) or statements of general principle. Undertaking a thorough examination and reappraisal of one aspect of our teaching would give us the chance to relate principles to a wide area of practice. Language, something which goes on in every lesson every day, was therefore a good place to start.

Making a start
The review was initiated (in January 1990) by the head inviting anybody interested to attend an initial meeting. This was attended by five (likeminded) teachers who between them could offer a range of expertise in language teaching and who, by good fortune, taught classes throughout the schools' age range. Other pressures on one member soon reduced the steering group (as we named ourselves) to four, though the age spread remained. The head also dropped out of the group after the first meeting.

At this meeting some basic principles were agreed. We would start from where we were, by examining current practices; we would make use of available expertise from within and outside the school; we would seek out and observe good practice, again both within and outside the school; we would build up an accessible collection of recent and relevant books; we would take into account the 'pervasive issues' and our 'view of the child'; we would test out interesting methods and procedures in an objective way and the final policy would be subject to periodic review. We all believed that the development of the policy should involve the active participation of all staff and we also accepted that we would need to be guided overall by a close examination of the National Curriculum. At this stage it seemed a simple and obvious decision to run the review in stages, one per term, in the order: oracy, writing, reading.

At the beginning we had differing views of the function of the review. While all were agreed on the need for a practical outcome, I, for example, saw the final policy statement as secondary in importance to the debates we would have as we formulated it. The head, on the other hand, placed some value on having a succinct statement which would be useful to any teacher coming new to the school and which could help us explain to parents and governors our approaches to language. (It soon became clear that for a few members of staff the policy had a third meaning, as a kind of 'test' on which current practice could pass or fail.)

We chose to start with oracy because we felt, rather naïvely as it turned out, that this would be the area where people would feel least threatened since we would all be starting on a roughly equal footing. We soon realised, however, that there is no area of the curriculum to which teachers come without any baggage. When you say 'We're going to develop a policy for speaking and listening', some people think of organ- ising for purposeful talk in collaborative group work; for others it may mean drama or oral story-telling; but there may be someone who wants to go straight to the important business of finding ways of keeping the noise down in the dining hall! During the spring term we held five staff meetings at which we discussed current practice, debated controversial issues, listened to tapes we had all made of our children talking and lis- tened to the Oracy Project co-ordinator.

By March, although (to my knowledge) no new teaching methods had been tested, a lot of issues had been raised and I think the general level of awareness of oracy matters had been raised too. If we had been suc- cessful in raising things, however, the steering group had to face the fact that they were all still up in the air. I got the job of assembling the most important of the things which had been said into a discussion paper, which I circulated to all staff. Then it was the end of term.

Developing a policy for writing
The term we had allocated to writing went in much the same way. We looked at children's work and opinions and held a number of lively dis- cussions. The structure for this work was partly provided by the National Writing Project INSET pack *Making changes* (National Writing Project, 1990). Again, we had stirred up a lot of ideas, but were still a long way from making genuine changes, and some people (including members of the steering group) were beginning to get frustrated by the apparent lack of focus and objective. Faced with having to decide

between summarising the discussion to date and allowing more time to work on writing, we opted for the latter course. In the first instance this was to be for a further term, but in practice it was to be a whole year before the review was complete.

One reason why we felt able to keep on with writing was that, collectively, the steering group had a fairly clear idea of what we wanted the final policy to contain. We all agreed, for example, that we should foster children's enthusiasm for writing and the development of their proficiency as writers by respecting the skills and knowledge that they already have, by listening to what they have to say and offering them support in their writing, but that we should still leave young writers with full responsibility for their own work. We believed that writing should be purposeful and addressed to a known audience and that our approach should be developmental, in the sense that we wanted both to foster children's development in the skills of writing and to bring them to see how their text developed through drafting and redrafting. A number of colleagues, including some outside the steering group, were already working according to these principles (sometimes termed the 'process model') and were keen that this sort of approach should be embraced by the final policy. Thanks to these people, there was already evidence within the school that a process model of writing could work. As well as drawing on this experience, discussions were informed by knowledge gained on short INSET courses (about half the staff managed to attend something on writing during the review period) and on visits to observe good practice in other schools.

It was opportune that at this time I was offered the chance, for the year beginning September 1990, to work as a floating teacher within the school. Suddenly my work for the review would no longer be limited to organising staff meetings, but could go on in classrooms other than my own. Done in a heavy-handed way, of course, this could have been disastrous. If it had appeared that I (a member of the senior management team) was being sent into classrooms to make sure that everyone was teaching according to the new policy (it would have been possible to assemble a policy statement at that stage), little of value would have been achieved. What actually happened was that I was given no specific brief at all, although I did express a wish to work with colleagues in their own classrooms rather than replacing them. I also expressed the anticipation that people would be interested in working on areas of innovation – which in the present climate would not necessarily mean writing. Not surprisingly, however, a number of people asked me to help them set up what had come to be known in the school as 'personal writing' (children writing regularly on their own subjects to produce pieces for publication in the classroom) with their classes. Gradually the number of people using – and talking about – a process model was growing.

Towards the end of the summer term we had, as a staff, looked again at the National Curriculum and at our own 'view of the child'. In the light of these, it appeared inevitable to most people that our eventual policy would be to support independent young writers according to the process model. A few, however, saw the approach as little more than a gimmick, while others, including some who were already using personal writing, had doubts or particular problems which they needed to resolve. It seemed that the obvious next step, and one which had majority support, should be to organise a pilot study of personal writing. This was to take place in the spring term of 1991.

After agreeing some ground rules concerning time to be allotted, children's equipment and their ownership of texts, we agreed the means of evaluation, which would draw on children's texts and the views and observations of both children and staff. It was stressed that all contributions to the evaluation were welcome and that the trial was genuine: it was not to be a backdoor way of imposing personal writing.

During the pilot study I was most concerned with enabling and encouraging the overlapping activities of sharing and reflecting on practice. This involved:

- Informal discussion – the value of this for the dissemination of ideas is often overlooked and in our context it had the additional benefit of allowing people to rehearse arguments for use in formal meetings.
- Questionnaires – addressed to teachers at half-term and towards the end of the project.
- An 'open agenda' staff meeting – having led many of the earlier meetings, I for once kept quiet and took notes.
- Interim reports – these obviously drew on all of the above, as well as on my own observations and on what I had learned from talking to children and reading their work. They offered an opportunity to highlight commonly held concerns and to share interesting and successful practice (and sometimes, of course, these two functions were connected). I always invited comments on and correction of these reports.
- Final evaluation report – this was intended to give all teachers a full overview of how colleagues and children had worked and to raise a number of questions which remained to be addressed.

All this created a circulation of information in which ideas were spread and refined by constant testing and discussion. The element of repetition had some benefits too in the context of what was to be, after all, quite a profound cultural change.

Once children had begun to develop their own writing, the momentum of their enthusiasm became an important force for change. Thus it was very easy to set up a school magazine, which was open to contributions from children of all ages and run by an impressively self-reliant group of year 6 children. An 'open studio', organised to allow children to come and read each other's work, became, spontaneously, a place where children chose to come (in their lunch hour) and write. One of the mooted shortcomings of personal writing, that children would be stuck for ideas and become bored, became hard to sustain in the face of such visible public activity. In this way some of the scepticism about personal writing – and this ranged from the healthy variety right through to evangelical incredulity – was allayed.

Looking back
Waiting until the very end of the review period before producing the final draft of the policy meant that its authors were able to look back and take into account not only the discussions held a year earlier, but also the actions which had been taken and the changes we had seen in our children over this period. I, for one, am confident that the review has brought about a genuine change in how, as a staff, we teach and think about language. I think the reasons for our successes must include the following points:

- We started from where we were. To do this it was essential to recognise that we didn't all start from the same place. Admittedly a very small (and over time diminishing) number took the line 'You can't get there from here', but most were genuinely (rather than charitably or dutifully) interested and open-minded. Some were looking for fresh ideas to use in their classrooms, others for a coherent focus to the diffuse elements of their previous practice. The needs of this majority were central to the review, since it was around these people that the new consensus was to be built. Implicit in all this is the inescapable fact that the real language policy – what actually happens – depends on the expertise and outlook of those who implement it. In a sense the policy has no real existence outside the teachers who have developed it.
- The review was based on action and reflection. After initial discussions in which our concerns were raised (or stirred up!), much of the review of writing can be seen as a piece of action research.
- The whole process was based on trust and sharing. Every effort was made to ensure that everybody felt able to contribute and knew that all views would be listened to. In fact some of the most sceptical contributions helped greatly to focus and refine the argument.
- The steering group was entirely free of class responsibilities. I know that I could never have produced all the questionnaires and reports, supported individual colleagues and stepped back to take an overall view if I had had all the pressures of running my own class at the same time. Of course opportunities such as the one I enjoyed are rare (and almost certain to get rarer), but without at least some release time being made available I do not see how a review such as ours could be successful.

with the head the possibility of producing some for all staff. If guidance exists, does it match the suggested list? What are the differences? Could you compile a list which incorporates both sets of guidance?

2. What procedures are there for monitoring the policy documents' implementation? How often are policy documents reviewed?

8
Schemes of work

In this chapter we will look at schemes of work for your subject area: what they are, how they are produced, and how you might use them. For this section you will need the non-statutory guidance document or other guidance documents provided for your country and for your curriculum area and also any documentation available from your education authority.

What is a scheme of work?

A scheme of work is the essential working document of classroom practice, relating to the nature of work to be covered during a year/key stage. It will embrace the requirements for the subject that are set out in the associated programmes of study. It should help teachers to plan and teach. It will reflect the broad principles laid down in the statement of school policy, and be largely concerned with details of knowledge, skills and processes to be taught during the year/key stage.

This document will probably be in two parts. One part gives an overview of the subject content to be covered in a period of time, and is linked closely to the National Curriculum. The second part may contain activities for teachers to use with their pupils. Both parts will show how to implement the National Curriculum requirements for a particular subject area and demonstrate that the coverage is balanced and builds in progression. The document will probably be put together for each year or class in the school; an outline of the major areas for each class will provide an overview of the curricular area in the school or in the key stage. The document may be available to parents and governors in part or as a whole. Both the writing and subsequent reviewing of a scheme of work should involve all the staff who are concerned with its teaching. These are very time-consuming documents to produce, and everyone must feel that they have ownership of the final document and should therefore support its implementation.

When planning any activity or scheme of work, the starting point will need to take account of the following issues:

1. The children's previous experiences, needs, skills, and knowledge. For this, you will need to consult the class teacher, records, and evidence, and you may need to initiate a short activity to make an assessment of the child/children's level.
2. The links between subjects, or areas of learning, and experience. Here, for instance, you will need to balance the requirements of a published mathematics scheme and the integration in topics of mathematics teaching and learning. Cross-curricular links with skills and themes should be treated similarly.
3. The National Curriculum requirements, POS, ATs and NSG.
4. Differentiation – so that pupils working at different levels can achieve success – either by planning different activities, or by differentiation by outcomes from the same task, or by receiving differential support from the teacher.
5. Agreed policies within the school for National Curriculum subjects and cross-curricular themes, special needs, assessment, record-keeping and school policies on schemes of work.
6. Each child's entitlement to a broad, balanced and relevant curriculum.

Martin Skelton, writing for *Primary File* (1995), suggests that a scheme of work sets out to ensure that:

- what children are learning is appropriate;
- teachers are using the most appropriate ways of enabling children to learn;
- the school is able to deliver what it has planned;
- there is a degree of consistency in the experiences that teachers provide for children. (Source: Skelton, 1995, p35.)

Read the section on planning schemes of work in the non-statutory guidance document, or other appropriate documents for your subject area. Make notes on the key areas that it is suggested a scheme of work covers, and compare this with the list already given, and also with the scheme of work for your subject area in your school.

There is no set formula for the exact components of a scheme of work, but there are some items that you would expect to find in most of those produced. Learning outcomes should feature in a scheme of work. These are the things that you want the children to learn; they may sound quite simple, but it is important to describe them clearly. The learning outcomes need to be clearly defined and written in such a way that you will be able to collect evidence of them being achieved. As an example of this, an outcome could be stated as: 'children will be able to describe the features of a house', or 'children will be able to explain the reasons for using a fair test'.

If you state the learning outcomes in terms of what children will know or understand, how will you be able to collect evidence of this occurring? The following is a list of suggested words that you could use when writing the learning outcomes, which would enable you to collect evidence of achievement: 'state ... describe ... give examples of ... suggest reasons ... explain ... evaluate ... pick out ... distinguish between ... analyse ... carry out ... summarise ... show diagrammatically ... compare ... demonstrate ...' This is not an exhaustive list and you will be able to think of other phrases. In order to check if you could collect evidence from such a written word, say to yourself 'Could I see/hear a response to this statement?' If not, then the phrasing needs to be changed. Although you may feel that some do not apply to the age group that you teach, try re-wording them and then testing for evidence collection.

Activities that children will undertake are also part of any scheme of work. These will enable the learning outcomes to be achieved and therefore the range of activities will be wide. They also need to take account of the requirement for resources and should be feasible within the school. They don't have to be completely new activities and can be taken from commercially produced schemes, worksheets or other appropriate resources. This leads on to the need to identify the resources needed as part of the scheme of work.

Included must also be some ideas of the pace and volume of work to be achieved within a given timescale. This helps when deciding on the sheer feasibility of completing the work. Schemes are not effective if half of the work detailed is not completed, as this creates difficulties for continuity and progression across the school.

Assessment must be an integral part of the scheme of work. It can be useful to think about assessment opportunities at the start of the compilation of the scheme rather than as a bolt-on extra. These do not have to be specifically generated assessment activities, although there may be situations in which this is the most appropriate strategy. It is worth checking across a scheme of work to see what evidence of attainment would be generated for the activities. Then, by cross checking this against the National Curriculum, any gaps could be identified and planned into the draft scheme.

Included in this chapter are a range of schemes of work, including some completed as a separate subject and some from a topic base (see Figures 26–31 on pages 120–25. You may find it useful to discuss the merits of both approaches. These are not the only formats and they will vary from school to school. Your LEA may have produced guidance for particular subject areas, or more generally, which cite either an authority's format, or again show a variety of approaches.

FIGURE 26 Student's planning of a scheme of work for science

YEAR 5 SCIENCE: SCHEME OF WORK

Class: Y5
Theme: Houses and Homes   Date: Sept 91

Knowledge and Understanding Focus
AT2 Strand (IV) Energy flows and cycles of matter within ecosystems

POS	ACTIVITIES	T & L	RESOURCES	AT1 FOCUS	OPPORTUNITIES FOR ASSESSMENT	SPECIAL NEEDS EXTENSION/SUPPORT
They should investigate how far everyday waste products decay naturally	Bury different types of waste	Discussion. T lead group practice. Group to report back to class.	Different types paper, metals, plastic, wood, foods (NB safety: no meat products)	Making predictions/observations over a period of time/comparing what is expected with what is observed	AT2 L2 d AT1 L2 abc	Sheet for recording observations Word bank
Key ideas – humans produce a lot of waste; food can be kept fresh in many ways.	How can we keep our sandwiches fresh?	Group	Different containers cling film, paper and plastic bags.	Predicting	AT1 L3/4 by outcome AT2 L5d	
They should investigate the key factors involved in the process of decay such as temperature, moisture, air and the role of microbes.	Using mould jar to investigate the factors likely to contribute to and accelerate decay.	Group	Mould jars, cotton wool, foods (NB safety not meat products; see also safety appendix on disposal).	Planning whole investigation		
Key ideas – decay can be affected by moisture, temperature. Ways of preserving food are.......... Microbes can be useful or harmful.	Preserving foods	Pairs	Cabbage, onions, fruit, etc, vinegar, sugar; salt.	Fair testing	AT1 3c 4b (as part of whole investigation)	Extension. Able groups investigate different strengths of solutions.
	Beneficial microbes – Talk from local dairy on milk hygiene.	Preparation of talk for class				Researching shelf life of products from labels. Letter to local supermarket about fresh produce and turnover.

FIGURE 27 *Maths scheme of work. Attainment Target: capacity and volume (level 1).*

STAGE	NC Ref	TOPIC	VOCABULARY NOTATION	ACTIVITY AND SUGGESTED APPROACH	EQUIPMENT	REFERENCES
1A	4.1.c*	Capacity		Practical		
		Introduce vocabulary	Full, empty, half, nearly, pour, fill, liquid, float, sink etc	Sand and water, play activities. Filling and emptying containers	Containers, sand, water, peas, rice, lentils etc	
1B		Extend vocabulary	Holds more, holds less, least, most, overflowing	As above	As above	
1C		Ordering & comparing objects		Order objects and explain reasoning. Compare the capacity of two containers	Arrow, cards. Holds less than------	
1D		Arbitrary measuring using non-standard measures		How many cups are needed to fill this jug?		
				Building regulations for schools		Links CV10
5C	2.5.d*	Converting one metric unit to another	cm^3, litres, millilitres	Practical activity to convert one to another	Measuring jugs etc	Nuffield 4 page 32/35 page 86/88 Nuffield 5 page 30 Ginn 6.2 page 20/21 Ginn 5.2 page 70 SPMG 4 page 109 SPMG 5 page 99/100
5D	4.5.d*	Formulae for volume		Know and use formulae for cubes and cuboids and triangular prisms		

* Part of NC reference

Source: Loughton Combined School, MK.

FIGURE 28 *Maths scheme of work. Attainment Target: algebra (level 1).*

STAGE	NC Ref	TOPIC	VOCABULARY NOTATION	ACTIVITY AND SUGGESTED APPROACH	EQUIPMENT	REFERENCES
1A	3.1	ALGEBRA Patterns	Continue, repeat, copy the pattern. What comes next? Make a pattern ordering, carry on	Pattern cards to copy and continue. Can you make up a pattern of your own?	Beads & strings, cubes, bricks, pegboards. Squared paper, gummed papers - logiblocks both 2D and 3D. (Plus any construction type apparatus.)	
1B			What's missing in the pattern?	In a pattern card - what is the missing part of the pattern? e.g. R B R ? R B = B is missing	- any shapes	

Source: Loughton Combined School, MK.

FIGURE 29 *Whole school plan, Olney First School, Bucks*

| | KEY STAGE 1 | | | KEY STAGE 2 |
	RISING 5s / RECEPTION	YEAR 1	YEAR 2	YEAR 3
AUTUMN	Theme: Subject elements: Maths: Science: History: Geography: Other:	Theme: Houses Subject elements: Maths: Shape, size, ordering, number, odd/even, data handling, time, pattern, tessellation. AT 2, 4, 5 Science: Materials and their behaviour. Naming and labelling, properties and characteristics. AT 1, 3, 4 History: Time line, Houses through Ages (Grandparents), Dr Barnardo. AT1, 3 Geography: Plans, maps, following directions. AT1, 2, 4 Other: Technology AT 1, 2	Theme: Lighthouse Keeper's Lunch Subject elements: Maths: Science: AT1, AT2 Food and personal hygiene; AT4 Forces, Electricity, Sinking, Floating; AT5 Heating, Cooling History: AT2 - Story of Grace Darling, Edison, Treasure Island - AT3 Books, Photographs Geography: AT1, AT2 Comparison of seaside/home; AT3 Weather, Rain cycle, Rocks and cliffs; AT4 Journeys and Transport & Purposes of Buildings Other:	Theme: Invaders and Settlers Subject elements: Maths: AT2, Strand 2 - Movement location; AT4, Strand 3 - Measurement Science: AT3 - Materials - Strand 1, 3 (Continued throughout the year); AT4 Physical processes, St 5 History: Core Study Unit 1; Supplementary Unit - Ships and Seafarers Geography: On-going AT1, 3, Weather Other: On-going Science - AT3 level 4, Strands 1, 4
SPRING		Theme: Toybox Maths: Coin identification, graphs, shopping, weighing, sorting - Venn, Carroll diagrams. AT 2, 3, 4, 5; Science: Forces, Magnetism, AT4 History: Time line (Toys through the Ages) AT1 Geography: Toys from different cultures	Theme: In the Air Maths: Science: AT1, AT2 Living in Space; AT3 Chemical changes; AT4 The earth's place in the universe, Forces, Gravity, Energy, resources, fuels History: History of Air Travel - Patch Study - 1960s (First Man on the Moon) AT1, AT2 (Interpretation stories, biographies) Geography: AT2 looking down on world maps; AT3 Satellite - use weather patterns; AT4 Journeys; AT5 Environment 'one world'	Theme: Toys Maths: AT4 Handling data Science: AT4 Physical processes Geography: On-going AT3 Weather; AT2 Skills
SUMMER		Theme: Animals (Minibeasts) Maths: Symmetry/Reflections, Tally charts. Simple multiplication and division AT2, 3 Science: Design a moving animal, life cycles AT2 History: Extinct animals, e.g. dinosaurs Geography: Habitats, human influences AT5	Theme: Minibeasts/Hedgerows Maths: Science: AT1, AT2 (Organisation of living things, human influence on plants, animals) History AT1 Changes in agricultural techniques Geography: AT1 Effect of weather on plant and animal life; AT3 Map - AT2 Land use; AT3 Map - design and make miniature garden; AT4 Use of land; AT5 Environmental. School garden	Theme: Local Study - Olney Out and About Maths: AT5 Handling Data; AT2 Shape, space, movement Science: Life and living processes, Strands 1, 2, 3; Materials and their properties, Strand 4 Geography: AT2 Knowledge and understanding of places; AT3 Physical geography; AT4 Human geography

Source: Olney First School, Bucks.

FIGURE 30 *Year-group planning 1*

ENGLISH
Topic book - starting school, school events, my friends, what we do in school, what we like best and least, people who work in school, animals in school
Order of the school day/week
School plan - where everyone works
Stories 'Starting School' - Ahlberg; 'Lucy and Tom go to school' etc
Poems - 'In the playground', 'Please Mrs Butler', 'My friends', etc
'Talk about sounds in and around school'
- traffic, playground

MATHEMATICS
Sets and graphs - number of girls and boys
Different sets within class - brown hair; blue eyes, etc
Ordering - height
Comparison of objects in classroom
- biggest, smallest
- heaviest, lightest
- longest, shortest
Order of school day, week
Times of school day
Sets of things found around school
Graph - transport to school; favourite colours

SCIENCE
Observation of school grounds and collection of items
- natural, made; litter
Materials used around school - brick, plastic, glass, tarmac
Textures
- rough and smooth
- rubbing
Sounds around school - inside and out

MUSIC
Sounds from around school
Favourite songs
'AT 1/4 past 3'
'Thank you for our friends'

HUMANITIES
Map of where we live - routes to school
Address and telephone number
History of the school
Changes - recent
Who we come to school with
Places we pass on the way to school
Location of school
History 1a, 1b, 2a, 3a

PE/DRAMA
Act out stories
Use of equipment in Hall
How to use it - safety and variety of use

TECHNOLOGY
Playground - how we could improve it
Word processor 'I like to ... in school'
Box plan of school and 3D models
Computer programmes - magazines

ART/CRAFT
Painting and drawing of school
Friend frieze/mobile
Brick/bark rubbing
Hamster collage
Paint 3D models
Teacher portraits
Uniform/hamster collage

RE
Our friends in school - what is a friend?
People who help us in school
How we can all help in school
Things I like to do in school

Source: Olney First School, Bucks.

FIGURE 31 *Year-group planning 2*

ENGLISH	MATHEMATICS	SCIENCE
'Show and Tell' sessions News/diary Book reviews Handwriting, letter formation and practice Phonics, sounds, blends Simple word building Silent reading Story tapes EAT 1 - 5 covered	SMPG work books and work cards Coins - coin recognition - coins up to 10p Recognition of numbers over 10 Number conservation Number formation Time - o'clock and 1/2 past Weighing - balance - measure } non-standard units	Observation of weather Care of school pets/classroom plants Seasons - changes - autumn
MUSIC	HUMANITIES	PE/DRAMA
Names of percussion - how to hold, how to play Percussion work - listening and repeating rhythms Clap rhythm - repeat Making sounds - body/instruments Quiet/loud, High/low, Long/short sounds 'Music Box' - BBC radio		BBC 'Let's Move' programme Large apparatus Skills with small apparatus Games with small apparatus Singing games/team games
TECHNOLOGY	ART/CRAFT	RE
	Christmas art and craft activities Binca canvas sewing Clay Cutting and sticking Paint/crayon/felt tip/tracing	Christmas story Christmas in other lands Care for others

Source: Olney First School Bucks.

You will notice that the examples given here show schemes of work over differing timescales. They either focus on a particular subject area only or cover the full range of subjects to be studied over a term. The format of the schemes shows the variety of ways in which organisation, approach and resources are used within schools. These schemes were developed prior to the Dearing revision of the curriculum and are included here in order to show differing starting points, rather than being exemplars or templates for developing your own. The difference between the Olney school and Loughton school raises a fundamental question of whether primary schools should develop schemes of work by subject or by topic.

Summary

In this chapter you have looked at different ways of formulating schemes of work and their content. Schemes of work can take very different forms, but essentially cover the same key aspects, from which teachers can plan activities. You should now be able to review the process of developing a scheme of work and consider the most appropriate format in order to make the information easily accessible.

Suggestions for the reader

1. Does your school/LEA provide any guidance for the production of a scheme of work? Does it provide clear guidance, or are there aspects that could be improved? Can you work with colleagues to produce coherent guidelines for schemes of work?

2. Develop a scheme of work for your subject, or for an aspect of the curriculum if this is appropriate. If you can, share your scheme of work with a colleague from another school.

3. What measures are already in place for monitoring and reviewing the schemes of work?

4. Think about the advantages/disadvantages for producing schemes of work from the subject perspective or through topics.

5. Look at the schemes of work in your school. Do they have a common format? It may be possible for you to talk to a co-ordinator in another school to enable you both to make comparisons, or you could also use the examples given here.

9

Working with colleagues

In the past, many researchers and writers in education have noted that primary-school teachers have traditionally seen themselves as being relatively autonomous in their classrooms, but as having little influence on the school as a whole: 'teachers first and members of a school's staff second' (Campbell, 1985, p20). Part of feeling and behaving as a member of a school's staff team involves seeing this role as being relevant to the children in your care.

Focusing particularly on your curriculum area:

- note down all that you value in terms of your colleagues' contributions to planning the curriculum and learning;
- what are the positive things for you in working as part of a team in your school and in your co-ordinator's role as the leader of the team?
- What are the negative points, or the blocks, for you in working as part of a team in your school?

You may find it helpful to use a technique called 'force-field analysis'. Make a note of your goal – in this case, team-planning; this includes the production, realisation, assessment, evaluation and revision of the plan – at the top of the page, and note all the positive forces that enable you to reach the goal on one side of the page, and all the negative forces on the other. Figure 32 (overleaf) provides an example. Use your notes from the whole-school planning section to help you.

FIGURE 32 *Force-field analysis*

Goal: whole-school planning through various groups and liaison

Positives (+)	Negatives (−)
1. Opportunity to establish continuity and progression	1. Insufficient time to plan effectively
2. Opportunities to share practice, attitudes and ideas	2. Difficulty of keeping up to date with materials and research
3. Establishing a sense of ownership of ideas among staff	3. Difficulty of establishing team work
4. Opportunity to explore experiences and expertise	4. Work completed at the margins of staff time and energies

- How could you 'unblock' or overcome the negatives? Write down some strategies to try, and indicate who might be able to support you. An example would be a colleague who feels that their contributions are not valued. The strategy would be to set up a situation in which the teacher can write their contributions onto a poster, or to encourage them to lead an activity.
- Share your concerns and strategies either in a school-based group or with colleagues from other schools if you can.

Many teachers find it difficult to think of ways of overcoming the negatives. Often, these are caused by lack of time and money or poor professional relationships, which are complex problems to overcome. Before you act on your unblocking ideas, work through the rest of this section. We will now explore group and team dynamics.

Being part of a team

Being part of an effective planning team involves recognising your own strengths and role and meshing them with the strengths of others. This facilitates professional development and deepens the whole team's familiarity with, and understanding of, learning across the curriculum. It involves being able to say when you are having problems, without feeling less of a professional for doing so. A project funded by the Education and Social Research Council found that in effective schools, 'a sense of security encouraged individuals to take risks in being open with one another' (Nias *et al*, 1989). Such openness depends on you being aware of your relationship with all the staff, as opposed to with individuals, and thinking of the school as a whole.

It also involves developing a much greater sensitivity to group processes. Colin Richards, writing about team work, or 'collegiality', as he calls it, involving teachers in primary schools, notes:

The development of collegiality has implications for the in-service educa-
tion of teachers who will need greater understanding of inter-personal and
group processes to participate effectively and has implications for the role
of heads whose basis of authority may increasingly rest, not on their for-
mal position, but on their skills in facilitating colleagues' participation and
in helping them solve problems and resolve conflicts. (Source: Richards,
1988, p20.)

But as well as there being implications for heads, there are also implications for each member of staff. Successful team work means being sensitive to your colleagues' perceptions and responses and awareness of
your professional relationship. A useful exercise in reflecting on your
current position and considering how to negotiate change is to consider
whether you think of yourself as relating to others, or whether you
expect them to relate to you. If your school is at an early stage in working
collegially, you may want to think about this on your own for now. But if
your school has a well-developed collegial approach, a useful way of
reviewing whole-school working practices can be to carry out such an
exercise together. Your response to the question of whether you 'serve'
or 'are served' can reveal a great deal about the state of collegiality in
your school.

A further aspect of working successfully within a school team is having school-wide goals. Where there are school-wide goals, there is
always a slight tension over the extent to which teachers can develop
their own interpretations of them. Differences in the ways in which individuals interpret school policies and approaches have implications for
team work. Some differences may be necessary (for example, where the
children's age demands a flexible interpretation), while others may need
to be negotiated. It is a question of finding a balance between what individual teachers are comfortable with, and what makes sense to children
in terms of progressive expectations. It is not an easy balance to strike.

Developing group processes at school level can also mean encouraging
one another to contribute to co-ordinator roles, in particular through
small-group, open-ended work in which it is much easier to progress, for
example, than through self-selected task groups or working parties.

Since 1985 the encouragement to draw up a school-development plan
(initiated by an LEA document in that year) has meant that, in many
schools, year-long planning of school priorities for developmental work
is now shared with all staff, parents and governors. To help you to analyse your own role in your school's team, and the extent to which your
school works in a collegial way, focus on your school's development
plan. Teachers in schools that have no development plan should focus on
the collection of school policies.

Getting started

It is important to see any work that is completed with colleagues as part of the total development process. For any subject area, the process will link in the following way:

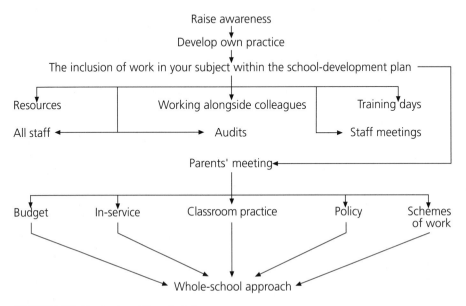

FIGURE 33 *Routes to getting started*

Working alongside or with colleagues in the classroom

By now you should have identified the skills of the staff and the needs of both the staff and the school and you are ready to start to work with colleagues. If you are starting with running in-service activities, then go forward to Chapter 10, and return to this chapter later.

The remaining part of this chapter will concentrate on working with colleagues in their classrooms, and your classroom.

To assist you in identifying a starting point, try to answer the following questions:

- Where can I begin?
- Who can I work with?
- What can I build on?

- What will my role be?
- What kind of initiative might I develop?
- What about the time? (Do I have release time or is this to be achieved at the margins of other tasks? Can I negotiate time?)

From gathering your data in Chapter 3 you should be able to identify a colleague with whom you could start to work, having carefully identified an aspect of their subject teaching that you could build on. Don't feel that you have to begin by working with a colleague who 'needs help'. In the first instance, it may be better to work with a colleague, or two, who is willing to develop their practice in your subject area. In this way, you, as well as the school, could be gaining from an initiative which should be successful, rather than one which might have lots of difficulties. Your role may vary, depending upon whether you are working alongside your colleague or they are working alongside you in your classroom. Ideally, a mixture of these would give you the scope to establish a trusting working relationship. Obviously this depends upon the arrangements that can be made to release either of you from class teaching in order to make such collaboration possible.

The kind of initiative that you might start to develop should begin with a small focus, e.g. a particular activity, a piece of equipment and its use, or an issue, such as extending tasks for a group of very able pupils.

Time is crucial in planning to work with colleagues. When planning, make sure that any arrangements are adhered to as far as is possible in a primary school. Meetings should ideally be at regular and reliable times. Working with colleagues can be a sensitive aspect of the co-ordinator's role. Arrangements that are changed without warning, or which are continuously altered, can damage any initial trust established, and this does not give a worthwhile initiative the status that it deserves. If problems of this kind occur, then you will need to go back and talk to the head to re-negotiate your role as co-ordinator and determine what is expected of you.

This starting point doesn't assume that the co-ordinator is the 'expert'. Because the co-ordinator has been given a responsibility for a particular subject area, then the expectation is that they will act as a facilitator in developing working practice. The co-ordinator may have an interest in the subject and be able to use the support of membership of a subject association and/or read about subject research and development.

When working alongside a colleague, you will need to consult them in order to plan a series of sessions. Remember to plan a manageable timescale into your ideas rather than something which is unrealistic. If this is the first time that you have worked in this way, you will want to plan outcomes for this work for both your colleague and yourself, and this can help to establish your co-ordinator's role within the school. If you achieve your agreed outcomes in collaboration with your colleague, then you are in a position to build upon this with other staff. You might wish to choose one of the following options:

- to take a small group;
- to work with an individual child with specific needs;
- to teach as a team with the class teacher;
- to take the whole class with the teacher as observer;
- to allow the class teacher to take a group while you take the rest of the class.

Remember to negotiate the choice and to be sensitive when working in someone else's classroom. From a base of working with one colleague, it should be possible to extend to others once an initiative is seen to be functioning well and to have benefits to the participants.

Lynn Churchill, a science co-ordinator in an Essex primary school, had been teaching for two years when she took on the role. She writes openly of some of the difficulties and the process of getting started.

> *My position as a fairly inexperienced teacher had made me aware of the need to become a 'professional friend', whereby 'I may have to demonstrate my skills but also be prepared to admit one or two weaknesses' (Harrison and Cross, 1994). If my role as co-ordinator is to involve monitoring and evaluation of science work across the school, then I need to build up my confidence to be able to gain access to other classrooms and work alongside teachers. I felt the need to establish attainable goals in my choice of in-service work. I needed to experience success and therefore chose to work with someone who is willing to develop their practice in my subject area. I believed it was important for me to choose something that I feel confident about ... In selecting this member of staff, I knew that she would feel comfortable with the focus and not threatened. Although she is more experienced than myself, I had to offer the opportunity for joint ownership of the project.*

Working with colleagues has benefits for you as the co-ordinator. You can gain knowledge about the way in which colleagues teach a particular subject area. This is professionally enriching, but it also enables you to gain access to the strengths and needs of your colleagues. The latter aspect will enable you to plan more effectively in your role as a subject co-ordinator. One co-ordinator wrote, 'I am aware that my role in school is gradually changing and I am gaining more status with experience.' If you are the teacher to be observed, this makes it possible to demonstrate a way of working, particular equipment, or any other aspect of teaching your subject that you have identified as requiring reinforcement. This may have emerged from either your audit of staff skills or your prior observations. Working with colleagues can also enable you to provide support for colleagues who wish to initiate, or want to try out, an aspect of teaching your particular subject area.

Co-ordinating change

The co-ordination of any type of change is not easy, even with chosen, manageable goals, when fully involving and consulting your colleagues, and with an awareness of the potential difficulties. Fullan's assumptions about educational change are worth reading in order to gain a clear perspective of your task.

1. *Do not assume that your version of what the change should be is the one that should or could be implemented ... Assume that successful implementation consists of a continual development of initial ideas ...*
2. *Assume that any significant innovation requires individual implementation to work out their own meaning ...*
3. *Assume that conflict and disagreement are not only inevitable but fundamental to successful change ...*
4. *Assume that people need pressure to change (even in directions which they desire), but it will only be effective under conditions which allow them to react, to form their own position, to interact with other implementers, to obtain technical assistance ...*
5. *Assume that effective change takes time ... Expect significant change to take a minimum of two or three years.*
6. *Do not assume that the reason for lack of implementation is outright rejection of the values embodied in the change, or hard-core resistance to all change. Assume that there are a number of possible reasons: value rejection, inadequate resources to support implementation, insufficient time elapsed.*
7. *Do not expect all or even most people or groups to change ... Progress occurs when we take steps (e.g. by following the assumptions listed here) which increase the number of people affected ... Instead of being discouraged by all that remains to be done, be encouraged by what has been accomplished ...*
8. *Assume that you will need a plan which is based on the above assumptions and which addresses the factors known to affect implementation ...*
9. *Assume that no amount of knowledge will ever make it totally clear what action should be taken ...*
10. *Assume that change is a frustrating, discouraging business. If all or some of the above assumptions cannot be made ... do not expect significant change as far as implementation is concerned. (Fullan, 1982, pp91–2.)*

Change is a difficult process and significant change takes time. So take heart from any small changes that you might have managed to implement as a co-ordinator.

In 'Successful curriculum change through co-ordination' by Harrison and Cross (1994), the authors suggest that in order for curriculum co-ordinators to become effective when working with others there needs to be a collaborative atmosphere. Only through mutual respect and understanding can staff value the expertise of others and be prepared to work with them. In order to undertake successful change, a co-ordinator must consider how much they know about the past and present situation and the opinions of the teachers with whom they will be working. (Some of this is covered in Chapter 3.) Also ask yourself how clear you are about the change required. What level of change will you be satisfied with? Are you willing to be fully committed to and involved with colleagues? Are you prepared to make changes? This process is likely to take some time, but you must retain your optimism and enthusiasm for the task throughout.

Working with colleagues does not have to occur solely in the classroom. It could include release time for you to visit other schools and centres in order to exchange ideas or to work on particular issues, such as transfer of information between schools, for your subject area. It could also include teacher placements and other available schemes. It may also include study groups or working parties. These need to have a specific focus and a fixed lifetime for that focus, with an end product in mind. An example would be to look at a spelling policy with a maximum lifetime of two terms.

Here are two examples of working groups set up for specific purposes as part of the development of subject areas.

Example 1
Marking policy, meeting over a period of six weeks to produce draft guidelines on marking for a particular subject area.

Example 2
A parents' workshop, meeting over a period of four weeks to produce a plan for the workshop, involving staff, parents and children.

Summary

In this chapter you have been introduced to ways of working with colleagues and to some of the issues involved. You may have tried working with a small number of colleagues in a collaborative way. You could have work in your notebook in the form of pointers for further work and evaluation notes from activities already carried out. You should now be able to establish a programme of work that needs to be undertaken. Armed with this, you should be able to negotiate with your head teacher the time necessary to continue your work.

Suggestions for the reader

1. Review your school's development plan in the light of your work in Chapters 3 and 4 on auditing staff and school needs. Are those needs reflected in the development plan? If not, then at the next whole-school review of the plan you could propose those additions to the priorities for the coming year.

2. Plan in outline the focus for a study group/working party with specific relevance to an aspect of your subject area. Decide upon the key aspects to be covered in six short, 'twilight' sessions, with an end product in mind.

3. Compare your experiences of working with colleagues with another co-ordinator. This may be within your school, or you may wish to choose a colleague working in a different context. If possible, choose two co-ordinators: one who co-ordinates the same subject as you, and one who has responsibility for a different area. Write down in your notebook any significant differences between their experiences, and say how this might inform your future planning of working with colleagues.

10
Planning and running in-service

In this chapter you will be looking at planning and running in-service for the rest of the staff. This is dealt with separately, as working alongside colleagues is very different from supporting them in more informal ways. In leading in-service sessions you are more overtly on show.

You may find it useful to look at Figure 34, which shows a procedure for in-service discussion focused on English. The headings used are general for all curriculum areas.

You will be looking at two different kinds of sessions here: a) using outside input from speakers or workshop leaders; b) using yourself as the major resource. Refer to Chapter 3 to review the possible areas of development of your subject area.

a) Using outside input

This situation is more likely for whole-day in-service sessions, but it would involve the same planning cycle as for 'twilight' staff-meeting sessions. Don't book a speaker at the end of the programme since this does not allow time for following up.

1. Check the finances so that you know your budget for this session.
2. Talk to a local adviser or similar to discuss potential speakers. This aspect is important if you have no direct links which you can use to gain information about the quality of speakers.
3. Before talking to a potential speaker you will need to have:
   a) a clear aim for the session;
   b) a range of possible dates (only one date is likely to involve trying a number of speakers);
   c) monies available for fees and travel costs incurred by the speaker;
   d) a provisional timetable for the day, showing the start, coffee, lunch and finishing times.
   e) before you talk to someone make sure that you know exactly what you want and where it fits into your programme of

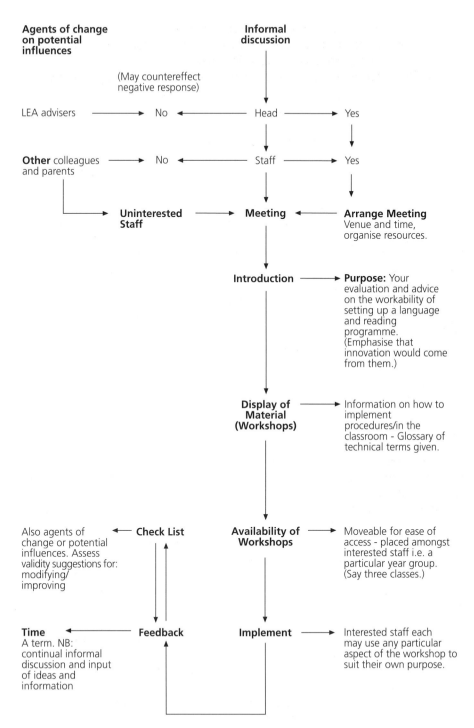

FIGURE 34 *Procedure for in-service discussion*

in-service, e.g. this may be the first session designed to get the series of meetings underway and you are looking for a stimulating and perhaps provocative start.

4. Once arrangements have been agreed and catering arrangements made (particularly important for a day session), you will need to prepare the staff. This may involve:
   a) producing posters detailing sessions;
   b) making sure that everyone knows what is going to be expected of them. Do they need to bring anything with them (e.g. children's work, or special clothing)? The check list in Figure 35 would provide a useful reminder.

5. Prepare an evaluation sheet, which should include questions pointing to future development from this session (an example is Figure 38, page 141). The important evaluation is the effect that the activity has on classroom practice and children's learning. Although this is an important aspect of the planning, any effects on classroom practice may take longer to evaluate.

6. Check equipment and room facilities and confirm with the speaker a few days before the session that all the arrangements are clear.

7. On the day:
   a) arrive before the rest of the staff and check the physical arrangements, put out a display to make the room look inviting, have the coffee/tea ready, and make sure that you can open windows for any necessary fresh air. Meet any speaker and make sure that there are signs directing people to the venue;
   b) make sure that the arrangements run smoothly, i.e., that sessions run to time and that all catering arrangements are as unobtrusive as possible;
   c) leave space at the end of the day for discussion/evaluation and thanking the speaker.

8. During the session, make notes on areas that you see as particular springboards for future work, especially if this is the start of your programme. Ensure that your colleagues are aware of, and can respond to, your list.

b) Using yourself as the major resource

You are most likely to be the major resource for 'twilight' sessions but also perhaps for whole in-service days.

1. Decide upon the aims of your activity.
2. Identify tasks which are suitable for the staff group and, at the same time, tasks appropriate for your skills as leader. You will need to feel comfortable and confident about using the chosen tasks.

FIGURE 35 *Planning and leading meetings*

Date of proposed meeting: **Leader/chair/facilitator:**
Start time: **Finish time:**   **Length of meeting:**
Place of meeting: **Participants:**

Catering arrangements and any special dietary requirements identified:

Title of meeting:
Purpose of meeting:
Prior publicity/readings/hand-outs/tasks prior to meeting:

Items to check:
Room prepared
OHP/flip chart/video/computer etc for leader
Other materials available for participants
Signs/posters
Catering organised if required
External/internal leader/contributor fully briefed and any fees agreed
Minutes organised if appropriate
Jobs/roles identified/allocated

At the end of the meeting:
Date of next meeting
Any action/jobs identified and allocated with time limits
Room to be cleared
Minutes organised and circulated
Any thank-you letters written to outside providers and fees paid

---

3. Try to have some idea of the knowledge that your audience already possesses. This will influence aspects such as the use of terminology and the actual tasks undertaken.
4. Be prepared to summarise DfEE, SCAA, TTA and LEA documents, either before meetings or as part of the process.
5. Decide on the organisation of the staff group whilst it is undertaking tasks, e.g. working in pairs, small groups or as a whole group. This may be decided by the size of the staff group, but it is worth trying to vary the organisation.
6. Decide on some likely outcomes from the tasks and check the coherence of the programme.
7. Think about the time taken for tasks and make out a schedule using approximate times.
8. Check the physical surroundings, equipment, materials and any documents required. Make sure that everyone knows what is happening, including non-teaching staff, who might be attending or should be aware of events taking place.
9. Leave some space at the end of the session for questions/

discussions and evaluation. An alternative check list appears in Figure 36, below. If you are not very confident about talking to groups, you can put a substantial amount of information on hand-outs. These can also be used to highlight issues for consideration before the next meeting/session. Figure 37 gives some guidance for the production of hand-outs which you may find useful.

10. Plan time for evaluation. Cross and Cross (1994) offer ways of thinking about this:

- focus on the positive and negative aspects of the session or the day;
- think about some questions for you and your colleagues to answer, for example: what did you get out of this activity? To what extent will you be able to implement this in your classroom? What are the constraints? How did you feel about the session/day, its pacing, timing and content? Did you get sufficient opportunity to offer your own ideas? Are you clear about the next step? How would you like to follow up this activity?

This information will be very valuable to you as you plan and negotiate for resources and time in the future. Do not take criticism personally: it will help you to improve your future INSET days/sessions. (Adapted from Cross and Cross, 1994, pp31–3.)

FIGURE 36 *Group sessions*

Date of proposed group session: **Leader/chair/facilitator:**
Start time: **Finish time:**   **Length of session:**
Place of session: **Participants:**

Catering arrangements and any special dietary requirements identified:

Title of session:
Purpose of session:
Prior publicity/readings/hand-outs/tasks prior to session:

Items to check:
Room prepared
OHP/flip chart/video/computer etc for leader
Other materials available for participants: hand-outs, writing materials, equipment for practical work
Signs/posters
Catering organised if required
External/internal leader/contributor fully briefed and any fees agreed
Minutes organised if appropriate
Jobs/roles identified/allocated

At the end of the session:
Date of next session if appropriate

Any action/jobs identified and allocated with time limits
Room to be cleared
Minutes organised and circulated
Any thank-you letters written to outside providers and fees paid

FIGURE 37 *The use and production of handouts*

The first questions to ask are:

- Why do you want hand-outs?
- What is their purpose?
- How many will you produce?

Once you have decided on the answers to these questions, then you can look carefully at individual hand-outs.

Are you aiming to cover background information? Are you aiming to summarise the main points of any area and to avoid participants taking notes at the time?

After this you need to consider the layout of any hand-out

- Handwritten or typed? Whichever it is, the writing needs to be legible.
- Balance between illustrations and text?
- Use of different typefaces or styles of writing?
- Use of headings and subheadings?
- Think about the readability and terminology used.
- Consider the layout on each page.
- Decide on choice of paper.
- How do the hand-outs fit in with the talk?

FIGURE 38 *Preparation of an evaluation sheet for any session*

When you plan any session, you also need to plan for opportunities for the participants to give feedback on the activity.

Areas to consider:
Room
Time
Catering facilities
Information received before session
Content
Have the aims been met?
Leader/chair/facilitator
Style of any presentation
Use of resources/equipment
Pace and general timing of activities within session
Hand-outs/tasks
What will you be able to develop within your own teaching?
Issues for future development

The examples given so far are for quite formal sessions, but it may be that you can contribute to meetings in a smaller or more informal way, for example, to:

a) provide feedback on a course;
b) introduce new equipment;
c) introduce an article or a piece of research;
d) provide a summary of how a particular recent change affects your subject area;
e) introduce a video of teachers/children engaged in a particular task.

Planning required before sessions

Planning is required for each of the above points, but taking e) introduce a video as an example:

1. View the video, note the time and video number of excerpt(s).
2. Note the issues raised.
3. Compile a list of questions to focus discussion after viewing, making enough copies for each viewer.
4. Make sure that the venue where you intend to view the video is suitable and that everyone will be able to see.

Rainey and Krause (1994) offer some starting points for INSET activity specifically focusing on geography. Starting points might be:

- persuading one teacher to discuss the geographical aspect of an activity or topic that they have carried out with children;
- watching a video together showing children working on a project, such as the BBC video, *Teaching today*;
- showing colleagues some work that the children in your class have been doing;
- inviting a teacher from another school to illustrate the geographical work that they have been involved in with their class;
- naming a country and asking teachers to tell you everything that they know about it. Write up these statements on a flip chart. Examine the set of responses together and search for evidence of stereotyping;
- collecting a random selection of books with a largely geographical content from the school library. Use the same search methods that you developed for the previous task to look for examples of stereotyping.

Workshops

The other type of session that you might wish to consider is the work-shop. These can take more time, not just to organise but to carry out, and therefore need very careful planning. It is easy to underestimate the time that participants will need to complete a given task. If you are running this type of session, you must remember that you are probably familiar with the tasks that you will ask your colleagues to do, and you must take this into account when planning the timing. The other thing that can happen if you have not run this type of session before is that you won't feel involved in the activity and so may bring things to an end too early.

When planning a workshop, the key areas are: the balance of activities offered; whether or not you have breaks between activities; how you enable feedback to the whole group; whether you are aiming for a specific focus or are offering a wide range of activities as an opening session to a series; and the space needed for practical tasks.

Sessions do not all have to be school based, for example, planning the activities for the local geography unit may involve you and the staff working in the locality, checking on the appropriateness of the activities planned.

Jacqueline Hambling, a geography co-ordinator, wrote about the planning that she undertook in her local area in Wiltshire. She arranged a time when all the lower-school teachers would be able to work in conjunction with the head teacher. She had given the staff copies of a large-scale map of the street which they would be studying; this was to clarify the purpose of the activity for the staff, and to give them time to think about the task. She had previously visited the area ... 'in order to compile the field-work activities but also to ensure that there were parking spaces, a café for a coffee break and toilet facilities'. From this field trip for the staff, activities were planned for individual classes.

There are some obvious advantages to varying the type of INSET sessions run in a school. Jacqueline expressed her feelings about how this event had worked as follows: 'I think that it was a very successful morning. We planned, in practical detail, work which would be the basis of our topic. It had been extremely enjoyable ... Even the simple fact of being able to discuss ideas in a relaxed and civilised way over coffee had enhanced the experience.'

Jan Bentley (1985) wrote of her experiences of developing physical education in a London primary school:

> *The chance really to introduce my approach to games teaching came in my second term, when the head teacher organised a residential weekend for staff to discuss curriculum initiative in three areas, of which physical education was one. I always enjoy practical sessions, so I decided to give a short demonstration lesson, in which the staff participated, followed up with a basic games lesson plan for both infants and juniors ... The*

weekend really seemed to break the ice. The staff seemed to warm to me and my approach.

Few schools can run to days away together in a hotel as a venue for INSET, but even on a limited budget it is possible to offer colleagues a variety of styles of presentation, ways of working and even venues for their work.

Ways of ensuring ownership of ideas in sessions

A crucial area is encouraging participants to feel that they own the ideas in INSET sessions. There are a number of strategies that you can employ to facilitate this process. A method of keeping track of ideas raised, so that individual concerns are not lost, is essential. This can be achieved through using a magnetic board with shapes which can be arranged in numerous ways. The shapes have ideas written on them and cannot be removed until the person who wrote the idea agrees. Ideas do not have to involve the use of costly equipment: for example, Linda Christian, a physical education and religious education teacher in a large primary school in Essex set up a washing line on which staff could peg their questions. The teachers' ideas could stay on the line until resolved or could act as a reminder of previous discussion. The important aspect is to gain the participation of all, even if not everyone says something in each meeting. The written record offers those who do not feel able to voice their ideas/concerns in potentially large groups an opportunity to express their views in a safe way, whilst still retaining ownership of the overall process.

Evaluation through the 'critical friend' approach

This is a technique mentioned by Williamson *et al* (1984), which involves using a 'critical friend' as a sounding board from which to obtain information about the quality of the course content, and the achievement of aims. This can be set up in a number of ways: firstly you could ask your 'friend' to give personal feedback after you have run a particular session; or, secondly, you could identify someone to provide feedback from the group, and this could be given formally as part of the session, or afterwards. If organised so that several people are involved, then you extend the participation within the group. On an individual level, you may wish to set up a mentoring or co-mentoring arrangement with a colleague with which to provide feedback and/or guidance specifically on the co-ordinator's role.

Summary

After reading this chapter you should be in a position to plan and carry out a number of different kinds of in-service activities. As part of your planning you will have decided on ways of evaluating your activities and will have collected evaluations.

Suggestions for the reader

1. Keep a folder of INSET ideas and resources for in-service work so that you can build up a bank of resources. Many subject areas have received INSET materials from the NCC and SCAA, which you may find useful for planning in-service sessions. Jot down your thoughts after attending someone else's INSET session. You cannot be expected to invent completely new ideas, but you can adapt ones that you have seen in action. You will need to modify any ideas suggested in the light of your knowledge of the staff group with which you are working, and the position of your subject's development.

2. Plan an in-service session for your subject area a) using an outside speaker, or b) run by yourself. You may like to share your thoughts with co-ordinators from the same subject area and/or from different areas. Note particular ideas/issues raised.

3. Plan a different type of session: either one mentioned in the list earlier, or one focusing on a particular aspect of your subject area.

11

Co-ordinating the co-ordinators:
the role of the head teacher

So far, this book has focused on the role of the co-ordinator as a separate task, and mainly for those whose primary responsibility is class teaching. In addition to this is the role of co-ordinating each of the co-ordinators across a school, carefully balancing the needs of the individual co-ordinator and the needs of the school as a whole. The following case studies show two aspects of the head teacher's role.

In the first, Susan Evans is the head of a small school in which teachers have a number of co-ordinating responsibilities. There are difficulties which arise from having part-time teachers on the staff and questions on how to involve them fully in the process. In the second, Ian Russell, head of a larger school, shows some of the work necessary to develop a monitoring policy throughout the school.

Case study by head teacher, Susan Evans

Context

I am head teacher of a two-class school in the south-western area of Wiltshire. The budget of the school allows the governors to employ two full-time staff, two staff who share one-and-a-half days, and a music specialist who works for an hour-and-a-half a week with all the children. There are occasions when the part-time staff work in the school for extra days. I have class responsibility for 21 year-two/three/four children aged between six and nine, combining key stages one and two. There are other year-two children in the other class. The part-time staff work with my class on occasions. It is crucial that as both head and class teacher I am fully aware of the curriculum opportunities being offered to the children by all the staff, for the following reasons: As head, I am responsible to the parents, children and governors for the quality of learning throughout the school being successful, and as class teacher, having a mixture of key stage one children in both classes means that it is essential there is continuity for the year-two children. The fact that other staff work with my class means that it is essential that we are all aware of the curriculum being offered to the children.

The role of the curriculum co-ordinator

If the co-ordinator is to lead the staff in achieving high standards, then it is essential that they are involved in the processes leading to an effective curriculum being delivered. In any school, it is necessary for the staff to take part in the co-ordination of the curriculum, perhaps making several subjects their responsibility. In a small school such as Hindon First School, it is even more important for all staff to be aware of this, and of the responsibilities and limitations of their situation. As head teacher, I must be sensitive to this and be able to lead even part-time staff in fulfilling their responsibilities. Each member of staff can bring their own subject expertise and knowledge to the curriculum offered and should be actively encouraged to do so. In my particular position, it is clear that all aspects of the curriculum are my responsibility, and this is the distinction between the curriculum co-ordinator and the subject co-ordinator.

Co-ordination of curriculum areas

The curriculum co-ordinator's role may differ from the role of the subject co-ordinator in many respects; however there are essential elements that are basic to both and in order to be aware of the curriculum offered to the children a complete overview must take place. The person responsible must be able to map the subject and find evidence of the learning taking place. They must also be in a position to evaluate the learning in order to encourage progression. Evidence will be found in various places, and in various ways, such as: visits to classrooms, discussion with the class teacher, discussion with the children, planning documents, children's portfolios, children's workbooks, work displayed, teachers' records and assessment documents. All schools have an abundance of these records; however, the crucial aspect of evidence collection is the time taken to collect it. Most staff who bear the responsibility for co-ordination are already fully occupied in their own classrooms. In a small school as Hindon First School all the staff have many 'hats' to wear and their time is often fully allocated. This leads to the important aspect of funding, which plays a large part in the way in which a co-ordinator functions.

Co-ordination at Hindon First School

As already outlined, the staff at Hindon are in a unique position. There are only two full-time and two part-time teachers, who have the daunting task of covering all the subjects and one-and-a-half key stages. They are in the position of having to support each other and to be aware that they need the support of the other schools in the area. Fortunately, there is a very good network in the locality that has already set up systems to enable subject specialists in both first and middle schools to support each other. This was set in motion in preparation for the arrival of the revised National Curriculum which, together with the reports by Ofsted inspectors, highlighted the importance of subject co-ordination in primary schools. This has proved invaluable already, enabling these specialists to lead a review of the documents and also to lead in-service sessions. However, the individual schools do have to look within their own structures to ensure that what they are delivering is quality education. As head teacher, I was in a position to instigate the process of co-ordinating the curriculum to ensure this was happening at our school. I was especially aware that it would be impossible to tackle too much, as success was essential for the self-esteem of the staff.

To put this into action for our school, I referred to the school-development plans. These had identified the areas of the curriculum that we needed to highlight this year. One of these was the language policy document, especially the written element, which the governors and I had identified as a key issue. Written into the plan was the ability to use a staff-development day and some supply time for a member of staff to audit written work throughout the school. This was extremely fortunate, as it meant that there was already the essential element of time and money allocated for the process. The other extremely fortunate thing about this development plan was that it identified one of the part-time staff as the person who would be responsible for the audit. This was the person who took my class for one day a week, who had several years ago been a head teacher of a small rural school similar to ours. This lady, although experienced, had not always recognised the full responsibilities of her post, which was for 20 per cent of the curriculum. She had lately begun to appreciate this, as she had become involved in an Ofsted inspection as part of the staff of another school in which she undertook the same role as at Hindon school. As a member of our staff, I was sure that the others would feel less threatened by her in the classroom than by a stranger. Previous in-service development days had been spent working as a whole staff, and knowing her as a colleague would give her the credibility needed. Consequently, there were many advantages for concentrating our efforts on to this aspect of the curriculum.

The process

Collection of evidence
To enable the audit, we had to set up the system with all the staff's co-operation. The criteria was firstly set by the evidence collector and myself. We discussed thoroughly the reasons for the audit, and set the parameters so that we could discuss them with the other staff. It was decided that the main focus would be written work. It was agreed that the delivery of the curriculum would feature as part of the audit; however, it was stressed that any feedback would be positive. When we agreed this, we both approached the staff to discuss the process with them. Although we all would find it stressful with someone watching us, I was particularly anxious that we should undergo the situation as confidently as possible. The whole staff discussed the situation carefully

so that everyone was clear in their minds as to the way in which the audit would be done. It was agreed when the auditor would be in the classrooms, and the staff discussed with her the pattern of lessons so that everyone was aware of the focus. Obviously, there would only be an element of language happening during the observation time; however, we were sure that this would be sufficient to debate after the lesson.

The date was set for the audit to take place on a Monday, followed by the staff-development day on the following Friday. I felt that it was essential that there should be feedback for the staff as soon as possible, in order to prevent unnecessary worry. The auditor gave a brief response to the staff immediately, and this was appreciated. Her experiences of the Ofsted inspection had guided her to do this.

The feedback
All the staff, including the educational-support assistant, were able to be at the staff-development day. This was made possible through the use of supply funding, and also the staff volunteering part of the day because they viewed it as important for the well-being of the children.

I chaired the meeting, and the lady who had carried out the audit led the discussion. We had previously decided that this should be done in a positive manner, and that all observations made would be connected to discussion with the member of staff concerned as to how the element of the lesson featured as part of the whole of the planning. This was to ensure that the points made were not in isolation and were in sympathy with the aims of the staff. As agreed, the emphasis was on writing and its presentation throughout the school. The discussion was semi-formal, but generally relaxed.

Once the general points from the audit had been highlighted, the discussion naturally led into establishing common practices. There was a great deal of common ground, which gave confidence to us all. Examples were noted to be incorporated into the general-policy document. It also became apparent that there were aspects of the curriculum and its delivery that needed to be debated. Particularly identified was handwriting. It was clear that a consensus was needed for all staff based on their expertise and experience. (The auditor had experience of a course led by Charles Cripps, whose 'Hand for spelling' is a resource that we use in school.) There were other aspects of language work identified for further discussion: a marking policy, the type of paper and lines used, the instruments that we use for handwriting practice, and the elements of the curriculum included under the umbrella label 'written English'.

The time that we had allocated for our discussion flew past, and before we ended the session I reviewed the process and our findings. It was very evident that we had just begun to scratch the surface. All staff agreed that further meetings would be necessary to enable us to cover all aspects that we had raised. Between us, we identified the areas that were most important, and agreed several dates for future staff meetings.

Evaluation of the process

Pressure of work

The staff that I work with is a dedicated team of teachers. They all put every effort into being extremely professional, ensuring that their planning and delivery of the curriculum is always the best that they can do. Their priorities are firstly, the children, and secondly, the school. This has been evident both in their approach and in the results that the children achieve. It is because of this that I was sure that the process would be successful; however, I was equally sure that it could go completely wrong.

The extreme professionalism that they showed meant that they were already working under pressure. Therefore, to ask that they should accept yet more work, and also allow their practice to come under the microscope, could have been the straw that broke the camel's back. The part-time staff particularly were already giving more than the time allocated to the school, either by spending more time with the children than they were paid for, or by attending more staff meetings than they were supposed to. The way in which we worked as a cluster meant that there were many 'special events' arranged for the children which all involved meeting together after school and devoting many hours to planning, etc.

Their input is vital and invaluable to the school, especially considering the size of the school and staff.

It was important to allow them to see that this responsibility was not just 'another thing' imposed from on high. I was most concerned that they should see it as an integral part of their profession, and that it would benefit the children and their learning opportunities.

There were two essential aspects of the process that made this possible:

  i the identification of the audit on the school-development plan;
  ii the funding of the staff-time for both the audit and the development day.

Both these factors gave the whole process high-level credibility. If the governors saw this as important, and not only recognised that but were prepared to fund it, then the staff afforded it the same importance.

Responsibility and self-esteem

The other main consideration I had was to enable the staff to feel their worth. If I had been the one to do the audit, then I think that they may well have had the feeling that it was something that was being imposed upon them by the head teacher. I was most concerned that they should not be put into this position, as we should take the pressure off them. It also served another important purpose. The auditor is an extremely good and experienced teacher, and has the respect of the other staff; however, there have been occasions when her assessment of her responsibilities has not been as broad as it should have been. So giving her the responsibility of the audit enabled me to reinforce the position that she holds as an expert, in such a way that she would accept the responsibility of the curriculum without feeling that it was not a part of her role in the school. The value of her expertise would be seen by all the staff and would be fully appreciated, while her self-esteem would be boosted.

Team spirit

I was also concerned that the staff would feel as comfortable as possible during the audit. This was the reason for the full and frank discussions we had before the event. I knew that they would need to be fully aware of the criteria laid down for the audit and would have to agree it. It was also made clear that I too would be under observation, and although this didn't take direct pressure off the staff, at least they knew that I was suffering just like them.

Staff development

Through the above process I was aware that there would be room for the staff to develop their professionalism. The staff discussion day also played a crucial part in this. Again, I would not be taking a leading role in the delivery of the day, though as chair I would be able to direct the discussion in the way that I felt was needed. It was important that all the staff felt that their contribution was of value, and that the agreement we reached would be through genuine understanding of all points of view. Again, the professionalism of the staff and the team spirit that we had built up over the years of working together ensured a successful and open discussion. There were many issues on which we agreed, and we were able to discuss and reach a genuine concurrence about several others. It was significant that all staff felt confident that we should continue the issue with future evening staff meetings. Even more significant was the willingness for other members of staff, with their own special expertise, to lead these meetings. This proves the value of the process in developing staff.

The future

We have obviously only begun to address the role of the co-ordinator at Hindon School. I feel that we have made an excellent start. This would not have been possible without several factors:

  i   the school-development plan, which identified the area to be highlighted;
 ii   the governors' recognition in that plan of the need for sufficient funds to enable it;
iii   the professionalism of the staff;

    iv   the expertise and experience of the staff;
    v   the team spirit of the staff;
    vi my recognition of the above, partly prompted through my studies on a co-ordinator course.

It is essential that the groundwork we have started is built upon during the next year. There are several reasons why it will be. The necessity of implementing the revised curriculum will drive the staff development for the next year. It will be essential that the staff work together in order to familiarise themselves with the new documents and orders. They will need to readjust the curriculum, and the assessment and record systems. In doing this we will be able to reaffirm the positions of responsibility of each person and, with the help and support of the cluster group, enhance the role of the co-ordinators. The recognition that the governors give through the school-development plans will be crucial. The process was given an excellent start because of the funding that had been allocated this year. Hopefully the value of this will be recognised and some degree of support allowed for the co-ordinator in the future. The whole process had been invaluable to the school, the staff and me.

Case study by head teacher, Ian Russell

As part of my studies on a co-ordinators' course, I evaluated the current position regarding curriculum co-ordination in Box Primary School, Wiltshire. My conclusion was that there was a great deal of work to be done if the subject co-ordinators were to be able to become effective in their roles. I outlined a plan of action for developing the role of the co-ordinator in the school. This included the following:

- An audit of staff understanding of the role of subject co-ordinator.
- A four-year plan of training to enable staff to develop their skills and expertise as co-ordinators. This would be based upon the model of developing the role of curriculum co-ordinator (see Figure 4, page 15), if agreed.
- A revision of the school-development plan to reflect the new emphasis. This would also include a new budget plan.
- Revised job descriptions to be discussed and hopefully adopted by the staff, which would reflect the increased expectations of their role.
- Guidance for the formulation of curriculum policy documents.
- A programme of non-contact time to be provided to allow each subject co-ordinator time to read around their subject(s) and undertake INSET, to write policies and schemes of work, and to spend time in colleagues' classrooms for supporting and monitoring the teaching of their subject area(s).

- It was also proposed that the role of subject co-ordinators in monitoring and evaluating the curriculum be further explored.

I intend to outline the progress made so far in implementing the plan, with particular reference to the work being carried out by the mathematics co-ordinator. I also intend to develop further how subject co-ordinators might be used in the process of monitoring and evaluating the curriculum.

Our progress so far

The following is an outline of the progress that has been made to date in enabling the teachers of Box Primary School to become more effective co-ordinators, and to become more involved in the monitoring process. It is difficult to set these activities in chronological order, because many took place concurrently.

In a series of staff meetings, staff undertook an audit of their curriculum co-ordination skills and experience using the following form.

FIGURE 39 *Auditing the role of subject co-ordinators*

'Can I do that . . . ?'

Skill/area of experience	Illustrate/evidence	Action/further development
Participate in policy/ scheme-of-work design		
Identify appropriate teaching methods		
Plan units of work		
Manage and lead other staff		
Teach alongside		
Negotiate		
Provide guidance and counselling		
Manage resources		
Evaluate/review policy/ scheme of work		
Provide formative support		

Source: Box Church of England Primary School.

Their conclusions were almost identical to mine: namely, that their role had previously been little more than that of resource manager. They also lacked confidence in their ability to provide support for other staff in their chosen subjects. They identified a need for more INSET and support if they were to be able to carry out their role fully.

I introduced a new draft job description, and was pleased that it was well received, in spite of the apparent increase in content, particularly with regard to the role of the subject co-ordinator. (A copy of this can be seen in Figure 3, page 12.) There was a clear acceptance by the staff that this was where we needed to go as a school. They acknowledged that much of what was contained in the document was already being carried out, but the need for strong INSET support was again stressed if we were to be able to develop fully as co-ordinators. I emphasised that I in no way expected teachers immediately to fulfil and demonstrate the full role and skills outlined in the job description, rather that this was our target over the next four years or so. This they accepted, and each subsequently signed the document by way of making a commitment to that process of development.

At the time that the above was taking place, the deputy and I took two days out of school to revise and update the school-development plan so that it would reflect this process (see Figure 40).

FIGURE 40 *Front page of a school-development plan*

Box CE Primary school-development plan: summary of objectives
Task complete

Ethos/philosophy	Start date:	Complete by:
i. **Mission statement, aims, objectives:** *Write, agree and implement in policies*	*Jan 1994*	*July 1995*
ii. **Whole-school ethos and behaviour policy:** *Write and implement*	*Oct 1994*	*July 1996*
Environment		
i. **Review current energy costs and investigate/implement possible savings**	*April 1995*	*Sept 1996*
ii. **Review play areas, swimming pool, outside storage**	*Jan 1994*	*Sept 1996*
iii. **Investigate/raise awareness of waste-disposal alternatives including recycling, cost reductions**	*April 1996*	*April 1997*
iv. **Write policies for: health & safety; asthma; medication**	*April 1994*	*April 1995*
v. **New dustbin shelter**	*April 1995*	*March 1996*
vi. **Improve hygiene/odour in boys' toilets**	*April 1995*	*March 1996*
Staff development		
i. **Develop policies for appraisal of non-teaching staff and staff/ESA liaison**	*April 1994*	*Sept 1995*
ii. **IT:** *Support/training for all staff according to perceived need*	*Sept 1994*	*July 1996*
iii. **Subject co-ordination:** *Review, revise and develop role of subject co-ordinator in school*	*Jan 1995*	*July 1998*

iv.	**Deputy head's role:** *Provide training for personal development*	*Jan 1995*	*Ongoing*
v.	**General staff development:** *provide training for perceived staff needs*	*April 1995*	*Ongoing*

Administration
i.	**Reorganise office filing system**	*Sept 1993*	*July 1995*

Curriculum
i.	**Maths:** *Revise policy; develop scheme of work & system of record-keeping; implement*	*June 1993*	*July 1996*
ii.	**Music:** *Implement Silver Burdett music scheme; reorganise resources*	*Sept 1993*	*July 1996*
iii.	**Health/sex education:** *Revise current policy in light of recent legislation*	*April 1994*	*April 1995*
iv.	**RE:** *Review and revise policy; develop scheme of work & system of record-keeping; implement*	*Sept 1994*	*July 1996*
v.	**Collective worship:** *Ensure provision accords with the law; write policy; implement*	*Sept 1994*	*July 1995*
vi.	**Special needs:** *Review/revise current policy in light of code of practice; train co-ordinator; implement*	*Oct 1994*	*July 1996*
vii.	**IT:** *Sort out software; set up class tool-boxes;*	*Jan 1995*	*July 1995*
	review and revise policy; develop scheme of work & system of record-keeping; implement	*Sept 1995*	*July 1996*
viii.	**Art:** *Enable teachers to plan to use art appreciation resources effectively*	*Jan 1995*	*July 1995*
ix.	**Revised NC docs:** *review new docs; revise SDP as required*	*April 1995*	*July 1995*
x.	**Topic planning:** *Plan new topic cycle (new NC docs)*	*April 1995*	*July 1995*
xi.	**Science:** *Review and revise policy; develop scheme of work & system of record-keeping; implement*	*Sept 1995*	*July 1997*
xii.	**English:** *Review and revise policy; develop scheme of work & system of record-keeping; implement*	*Jan 1996*	*Dec 1997*
xiii.	**History/geography/technology:** *Revise policies; develop schemes of work & system of record-keeping; implement*	*Sept 1996*	*July 1998*
xiv.	**Music/art/PE:** *revise policies; develop schemes of work & system of record-keeping; implement*	*Sept 1997*	*July 1999*

Community links
i.	**Church links:** *increase participation between local churches and the school*	*Sept 1993*	*Ongoing*
ii.	**Community links:** *Investigate existing links and possible developments*	*Sept 1993*	*Jan 1996*
iii.	**Cross-phase liaison:** *(a) create a greater match between Y6 & Y7 Teaching Learning Styles*	*Sept 1994*	*July 1996*

	(b) increase effectiveness of transfer dialogue and procedures	June 1995	July 1996
iv.	**Cross-phase liaison:** *Review and develop liaison with play-groups, and reception induction*	Sept 1994	Ongoing

Source: Box Church of England Primary School.

An action plan for the development of the subject co-ordinator's role was also written and both were discussed and agreed by staff (see Figure 41).

FIGURE 41 *Individual action plan for developing the role of subject co-ordinator*

Date: ***March 1995***

Objectives:
> *To enable each member of the teaching staff to become confident and competent in their role as subject co-ordinator.*
> *To enable them to develop knowledge and expertise in their subject specialisms.*
> *To enable them to catalogue, purchase and manage resources for their curriculum areas.*
> *To enable them to provide in-class support for other colleagues when teaching their subject.*
> *To enable them to begin to develop a curriculum-monitoring role within their subject area.*

Success criteria:
> *Each member of staff able to confidently lead INSET and provide advice and support to colleagues within their areas of curriculum responsibility.*
> *Resources catalogued and managed efficiently.*
> *Each co-ordinator given time out of their own classroom to enable them to undertake the action set out below.*
> *Co-ordinators spend time in each class supporting and monitoring their subject.*

What action is required:
> *Timetable for 1995–6 drawn up by HT.*
> *Teachers undertake personal INSET where possible.*
> *Each teacher to be released for **1 day** in summer 1995 to review new NC docs and resource provision for their subject areas, and prepare a submission for staff meetings.*
> *Each teacher to be released for **2 days** to review, sort and catalogue subject resources, to read around their subject and to write subject policy and scheme of work.*
> *Each teacher to lead a series of staff meetings to review/revise policy and scheme of work.*
> *Each teacher to plan for the implementation of that policy and scheme of work.*
> *Each teacher released for **2 days** to spend $\frac{1}{2}$ day MAST (Monitoring and Support Time) in each class, supporting subject teaching and acting as critical friend.*
> *Staff to review and develop monitoring role for co-ordinators.*

Who is responsible?	*IKR*	
Who is involved?	*Teaching staff*	

Finance/INSET/resources:	Budget source:
INSET:	*GEST/training*
TEACHER RELEASE in 1995–6: 20 days in total (approx. £1,500 supply plus HT cover)	
	LEA Initiatives

Completion by: *1998*	Report to: ***Governors***

Evaluation: Who? *IKR*	How? *Whole-staff review*	When? *1996; 1997; 1998*

Evidence from evaluation:

Outcomes for future plans:

Source: Box Church of England Primary School.

As part of the process of setting the school budget, staff were asked to draw up a request list of preferred INSET requirements from the county provision. This was to be based on the school-development plan as well as on their own perceived needs. Their requests were prioritised and a budget was set aside to cover both INSET and the implementation of the plan. The bulk of this budget would be the cost of supply cover for staff's non-contact time. Within the fiscal constraints, INSET was chosen that would allow staff to develop their subject knowledge as far as possible.

In addition, a timetable was drawn up for staff non-contact time within the financial year, centred around the action plan.

A draft religious-education policy was drawn up, using the guidance document (see also Figure 25, page 108). This was offered to staff as a model upon which to base other policy documents when they came to write them.

FIGURE 42 *Religious-education policy*

This policy document has been developed through consultation involving the staff and governors of Box School. It is subject to future review under the timetable laid down in the school-development plan. Its implementation will be monitored by the subject co-ordinator in consultation with the head teacher.

Associated documents: The Wiltshire Agreed Syllabus, Scheme of Work for RE
1.   Religious education and the school's aims and ethos
    1.1   In the statement of aims and objectives, under the heading 'Spiritual Development', we have stated that we aim to 'make each child aware that

every individual has both a physical and a spiritual dimension to their being'.

1.2   We seek to do this in an environment which is 'happy and relaxed, yet stimulating and thought-provoking, in which the children can enjoy learning and develop such qualities as kindness, tolerance and enthusiasm'.

2.   Philosophy

2.1   Religious education is concerned with making pupils aware of experiences and concepts basic to all religion. It is also concerned with investigating the visible features of particular religious and non-religious belief systems. It must go deeper, however, evoking sympathetic appreciation of the meanings and values enshrined within the systems.

2.2   Through religious education and other subjects, as well as in school assemblies, pupils can be helped to reflect upon those aspects of human life and the natural world which raise questions of ultimate meaning and purpose, and to recognise the spiritual dimension of experience.

3.   Aims

3.1   To assist pupils in their own search for meaning and purpose in life by examining those aspects of human experience which give rise to fundamental questions about beliefs and values.

3.2   To provide pupils with knowledge and understanding of Christianity and two other major religious traditions represented in contemporary British society, namely Judaism and Islam.

3.3   To foster in children an appreciation of their spiritual and cultural heritage.

3.4   To encourage in children a sense of awe and wonder.

3.5   To help pupils acquire the skills that develop spiritual awareness:

- observation;
- investigation;
- language;
- reference;
- reflection;
- empathy;
- questioning;
- discernment.

3.6   To promote in children a tolerance and sensitivity towards those with beliefs different from their own.

3.7   To help children make moral choices.

4.   The legal context

4.1   All schools are required by law to teach the Basic Curriculum, which comprises the National Curriculum and religious education.

4.2   The syllabus for RE in all county and controlled schools is determined by the local Standing Advisory Council for Religious Education (SACRE). However, in controlled schools, if parents so request, arrangements should be made for RE to be provided for their children in accordance with any existing trust deed, or the practice followed before the school became controlled. (Education Act; 1944.)

4.3   The 1988 Education Act requires all syllabuses to 'reflect the fact that the religious traditions in Great Britain are in the main Christian whilst taking account of the teaching practices of the other principal religions represented in Great Britain'.

4.4   The 1944 Education Act states that agreed syllabuses must be non-denominational.

4.5   Parents have the right to withdraw their children from religious education.

4.6   Teachers cannot be required to teach RE.

5.   Content

5.1   Religious education in Box School is taught according to a scheme of work based upon the Wiltshire Agreed Syllabus. This divides RE into two profile components and five attainment targets.

5.2   RE will be taught primarily from the perspective of Christianity.

5.3   The component of study dealing with other faiths will be undertaken by examining aspects of Judaism at key stages 1 and 2, and Islam at key stage 2. The other principle religions, namely Sikhism, Hinduism and Buddhism, will not be addressed, except in the context of class topic work or discussion.

5.4   In both key stages 1 and 2 the introduction of children to different aspects of religion should include meetings with people for whom this dimension of life is important, as well as exploration of a range of writings, artefacts, music, buildings, pictures, photographs and religious practices.

6.   Equality of opportunity

6.1   All children have the right to equal opportunities in religious education irrespective of gender, race, background or ability.

6.2   The beliefs, views and value systems of all children and their families should be respected and valued.

7.   Planning

7.1   It is recommended that 36 hours per year should be devoted to RE at key stage 1, and 45 hours per year at key stage 2 (The National Curriculum and its assessment; final report; Sir Ron Dearing, 1993).

7.2   All planning for RE should take place in the context of a whole-school strategy to ensure proper continuity, progression and coverage.

7.3   Some RE may fit naturally into the framework of class topics or arise from collective worship and/or assembly activities, but much will need to be addressed discretely or in RE mini-topics.

7.4   Teachers should ensure within their yearly or two-yearly plan for each class that attention is given to both profile components and all five attainment targets outlined in the Wiltshire Agreed Syllabus. Termly and weekly forecasts should demonstrate this coverage.

7.5   Coverage of RE attainment targets should be planned primarily from the perspective of Christianity. When other religions are studied, they should be taught in a way that clearly defines them as faith systems that are distinctive from Christianity, preferably by means of discrete mini-topics, or sub-topics of cross-curricular studies. This allows children to understand the special nature and features of each religion and to compare and to contrast them. It is hoped by this means to help children to develop a respect of, and tolerance for, people who hold other faiths and creeds, by giving them a greater understanding of the distinctiveness of each faith and its importance to its adherents.

7.6   Stories from other faiths should be used within the context of the study of those faiths, and not introduced randomly throughout the year. If they are introduced at other times, their religious source should be clearly identified so that they are distinguished in the minds of children from those that are to be found in the Bible, or as coming from Christianity.

7.7   Teachers should demonstrate in their planning that they have provided work for the children that is differentiated according to need. This might be done by differing either the tasks set or the expected outcomes. When planning, as much attention should be given to extending more able children as is given to providing for those that are average or below average in ability.

7.8   In their planning, teachers should look for ways of addressing cross-curricular themes that are relevant in the context of RE. These might include environmental, moral or social issues. They should also plan to take advantage of the opportunities that RE presents for using information technology.

7.9   In RE teachers should plan for a balance between different types of activities and different methods of recording the work carried out by the children. These might include circle time, discussion, art work, written work, tape recordings, drama, use of the computer etc.

8.   Classroom management and organisation

8.1   Different approaches to teaching and learning will be used, depending on the task and/or planned outcome. These might include whole-class, group or individual activities. A range of didactic and/or discovery methods may be used as is considered appropriate by the teacher to enable children to acquire information.

8.2   Tables may be laid out in groups or individually, as the task or activity requires.

9.   Resources

9.1   Guidance for the teaching of RE can be found in the 'Programmes of study and attainment targets' and the accompanying 'Support materials' published by Wiltshire SACRE.

9.2   These and other resources for RE, such as books, videos and artefacts, are stored centrally in the resources room. When used in the classroom, resources should be stored or displayed in such a way as to encourage independent use by the children.

9.3   **Religious artefacts should be treated with great respect and deference, in order to avoid giving offence to members of the faith community by which they are used.** (Guidance on the borrowing and use of artefacts can be found in the Wiltshire SACRE 'Booklist and artefact list'.)

9.4   Use should also be made of primary resources that are close at hand, such as the local churches and vicar. Members of faith communities may be invited into school to talk about their beliefs.

9.5   The management, organisation and budgeting for resources shall be the responsibility of the RE co-ordinator, in consultation with the head teacher.

10. Assessment, record-keeping and evaluation

10.1   All work carried out by the children should be marked in line with the school's marking policy.

10.2   Teachers should keep records which demonstrate that the children have completed the task or activity set.

10.3 Samples of work should be set aside for inclusion in the child's record of achievement and assessment folders, as determined by the school's assessment policy.

10.4 Past topic webs and details of RE curriculum coverage should be passed on to the next teacher on transfer to a new class.

10.5 The subject co-ordinator will be responsible for evaluating and reporting to the head teacher concerning the provision of RE throughout the school. This will require access to teacher planning and records.

11. Professional development and training

11.1 All staff will be given the opportunity to undertake training in the teaching of RE. This will be co-ordinated by the subject co-ordinator in line with the school-development plan.

12. Liaison with outside bodies

12.1 The subject co-ordinator shall liaise as necessary with outside bodies, such as the Diocese of Bristol, Wiltshire SACRE, the Foundation Governors, parents, and other parties with an interest in the delivery of the RE curriculum in Box School.

Source: Box Church of England Primary School.

A model for a scheme of work was not presented, as it was recognised that its format would vary according to subject.

As we have proceeded, it has become apparent that one of the biggest constraints upon this process is time. Teachers have an enormous workload and, if they are not to become overloaded, the rate of development has to be carefully considered. The senior management team has been fully involved at each stage of the process, and one of its roles has been to monitor carefully the pace at which we proceed, to ensure that staff are not overwhelmed.

Developing the role of mathematics co-ordinator

Whereas the previous section deals with the task from the perspective of the head teacher, this section will show how the mathematics co-ordinator has begun to develop a co-ordinating role.

The background

In 1993, the teachers working in the school were very concerned about the mathematics programme. Through staff-room conversations and through my monitoring of their weekly plans, it had become clear that they were unhappy with the current scheme. The children at that time were using 'Peak Mathematics'. All the children worked at their own pace on individual programmes, resulting in teacher overload. There was never enough time for teaching, and staff would often have to cover the same teaching points many times during the course of a week. In addition to this, the teacher in class 1 was finding that the youngest children demanded a great deal of attention when using the work cards. At this time the mathematics co-ordinator, a part-time teacher, agreed to attend a 20-day mathematics course because she felt very insecure in the subject. On her completion of the course she was very excited by her work and was eager to experiment with investigations and to support other staff as well.

I approached her with a view to her taking over the responsibility for mathematics in the school, and she was delighted to be able to do so. She then proceeded to lead a full review of mathematics, as follows:

- In a series of staff meetings the staff carried out an audit of mathematics teaching in school. This highlighted the need for both a new core scheme and a new approach to teaching mathematics.
- The co-ordinator researched all the schemes then available and, together with the staff, it was agreed that we would purchase 'Ginn Mathematics' workbooks to supplement the infant scheme, and 'Cambridge Mathematics' for the juniors.
- A new approach to teaching was adopted, in which teachers organised their classes into ability groups and planned mathematics topics that would be undertaken by the whole class, with each group working on differentiated activities within the topic. This resulted in a better use of teacher time and resources.
- At this time the co-ordinator provided support and ideas for colleagues concerning appropriate activities and investigations.
- She then identified the need for a full scheme of work which would provide a progression of work through each year group, thus avoiding repetition and also assisting in planning, recording, record-keeping and assessment. The development of this scheme was outlined in an action plan that she drew up (see Figure 43).

FIGURE 43 *Individual action plan for maths*

Date: *December 1995*

Objective: *To produce a scheme of work for the whole school.*

Success criteria: *A workable scheme is produced that is agreed by all staff.*
    New resources (i.e. Ginn and Cambridge) are introduced and
    implemented into the scheme.
    The scheme of work is typed and circulated.
    A programme for implementation is prepared.

What action is required:	**Date:**	**Action:**
• *Organise scheme-of-work format to take account of new NC ATs.*	*Dec–Jan 95*	*AdF*
• *Staff meeting to sort ATs from new NC doc; discuss how AT1 is to be included in the scheme*		

of work; consider how changes are to be recorded on the current format of scheme of work.	*25/01/95*	*Whole staff*
● *Whole-day meeting (JK/HW) to sort progression in KS1.*	*31/01/95*	*KS1 staff*
● *Non-contact time for AdF to review work on KS1 and devise starting points for KS2.*	*7/02/95*	*AdF (NS-L cover)*
● *Whole-day meeting (PH/AdF/NS-L) to sort progression in KS2.*	*16/02/95*	*KS2 staff*
● *Consultation with head teacher.*	*March*	*AdF*
● *Typing of scheme of work.*	*March*	*AdF/WJ*
● *Staff meeting to agree final document.*	*15/03/95*	*AdF*
● *Programme of staff meetings to implement (to be planned separately).*	*1995–6*	*AdF*

Who is responsible?	*Ann de Fleury*
Who is involved?	*Teaching staff*

Finance/INSET/resources:	**Budget source:**	
One day supply cover for AdF on 7/2/95	**£75**	*Supply*

Completion by: *March 1995*	**Report to:** *IKR*

Evaluation:	**Who?** *AdF/IKR + staff*	**How?** *Staff audit*	**When?** *1997*

Evidence from evaluation:

Outcomes for future plans:

Source: Box Church of England Primary School.

● Example schemes were obtained and examined by the staff. Finally, a model progression was adopted and a series of working parties set up under the co-ordinator's supervision to adapt the progression for our own use. The progression was cross-referenced to the resources available in school.

This is the stage that we have now reached. From here on the following is planned:

● under the schedule, the co-ordinator will prepare the draft scheme of work for typing;
● she has already begun to draft the policy, and is involving the staff in its development through staff meetings;

- when the policy and scheme are in place, staff meeting time will be set aside to discuss how they will be implemented, and the co-ordinator will be released to work alongside colleagues to assist that process.

Funding for the purchase of the scheme and for supply cover of non-contact time has been provided by using money from our devolved budget for LEA initiatives.

Developing the monitoring role of the subject co-ordinator
In this section I shall examine why monitoring is important, and how subject co-ordinators might be used to assist the process.

A rationale for monitoring and evaluating the curriculum
There is evidence to suggest that monitoring is poorly carried out in many schools. While it is recognised that most head teachers visit classrooms on a daily basis, it has been found that few engage in a structured monitoring process that seeks to evaluate the curricular strengths and weaknesses of the school as a whole, or that they deal with inconsistencies in teaching.

The importance of the task is recognised by all. The problem comes in seeking to develop a monitoring process which is both manageable and effective, but which does not overload the management of the school. Subject co-ordinators must be involved in such a system.

The following has been suggested as a rationale for monitoring and evaluating the curriculum:

- to ensure that the education of each child is as effective as possible;
- to ensure that each teacher is developed to their true potential;
- to ensure that the school can plan for its development on the basis of real evidence;
- to satisfy the need to be accountable;
- to feed a culture of openness rather than a culture of criticism.

Monitoring will:

- identify strengths and weaknesses;
- ensure management efficiency and value for money;
- feed future action.

Prerequisites for monitoring
Before effective monitoring can be carried out a clear set of aims and objectives for the school generally must be in place, and, based on these, an agreed policy for the subject or aspect being evaluated. Without these there can be no basis for evaluation. A scheme of work which clearly demonstrates a learning progression would also be enormously valuable.

All staff will need to have been involved in drawing up these documents, and subject co-ordinators will have a particular role in developing the policies and schemes of work with the staff. These documents can then be used to draw up aides-mémoire to assist in the process of observation and evaluation. For example, the co-ordinator may refer to the subject policy to consider how the classroom should be organised, what sort of teaching strategies should be expected, how marking and record-keeping is carried out, and so on. This will then inform their evaluation of how effectively the policy is operating throughout the school.

The school will need to operate an agreed approach to planning. This may take the form of standardised planning sheets, or an agreed content. This is important if we are to ensure that each member of staff is including in their planning documents the information that will be required for the effective monitoring of such aspects as balance and coverage within the curriculum, progression and differentiation.

This planning will need to contain long-term goals, which will include an outline of work and attainment targets to be covered (e.g., topic webs and a more detailed progression), weekly planning giving an overview, and daily/task planning which demonstrates the social context for learning (how the children will be grouped), and details of the planned activities and necessary resources. It would be helpful to both the teacher and those monitoring if there was also a place for some level of self-evaluation within the planning process, to be carried out after the activities are completed.

There will need to be an agreed system of marking, recording and record-keeping. These records will contain details of the results of both formative and summative assessment activities, and also objective observations by teachers and others. Information from these elements will be used to help assess the success of the learning activity and the effectiveness of each child's education, and also for providing comparative data. Pupils' portfolios containing moderated evidence of pupil achievement will offer further support to the monitoring.

How monitoring may be carried out

The following are some suggested ways in which monitoring might be carried out:

- monitoring of planning folders;
- structured and focused classroom observation;
- working alongside colleagues;
- the sampling of children's work.

How subject co-ordinators might be involved in this process

It would be impossible to monitor constantly every aspect of the curriculum simultaneously. Time and financial constraints would prohibit this. However, subject co-ordinators could play a significant part in this monitoring role if the exercise was properly planned. The following is an outline of a strategy which will allow this to develop. As part of the school-development plan, an initial area of focus within the subject under review is agreed. This will need to be fairly narrow for the evaluation to be effective. It may be chosen from a list of possible foci which are selected and prioritised, or it may be a single aspect that is felt to be important at the time. Within English, for example, this might be: the development of handwriting or poetry throughout the school, how effectively speaking and listening is assessed, how effectively work is differentiated for pupils of different ability, and so on.

From the policy documents, programmes of study, schemes of work etc, the subject co-ordinator might draw up an aide-mémoire of what should be expected. This could then be discussed with the staff.

In their planning, staff would be asked to give particular attention to the area of focus. If appropriate, sample lessons might be discussed with the co-ordinator and then observed and/or supported by them in practice. Outcomes could then be evaluated against National Curriculum-level descriptors, or compared with previously recorded planning activities or outcomes.

From this it should be possible to identify training and resourcing needs and/or future teaching/learning requirements.

This model in practice

As part of my recent appraisal of a head teacher colleague, this process was trailed. The head teacher in question wished to focus on the effectiveness of her monitoring of the curriculum. It soon became apparent to her that whereas informal monitoring was taking place all the time, formal monitoring was not established, and co-ordinators had no role in it.

A model for involving the co-ordinators in monitoring was therefore decided upon. Each co-ordinator would be involved with a non-specialist colleague in planning a model lesson. They would attend the lesson, observe the outcome and then evaluate it against the aims of the lesson with other colleagues in a subsequent staff meeting.

All three teachers found the experience to be extremely worthwhile. Their understanding of how they might become more involved in monitoring grew, and the value of such a process in the development of the school was put beyond dispute when they unanimously agreed to repeat the activity at least termly, budget permitting.

Conclusion

I recognise that we have a long way to go before all of this is implemented in Box School. However, we have set ourselves several years in which to achieve our goal, and, barring too many staff changes, I am optimistic that we can achieve our aim.

Summary

The role of the head teacher is crucial in the process of initiating and continuing the professional development of both the school and the individual co-ordinators.

Terry Williamson *et al* (1984), writing about curriculum leadership in physical education, suggest a development strategy for the in-service training of curriculum leaders. This strategy assumes four levels of involvement and dissemination:

- first level – head teachers;
- second level – curriculum leaders;
- third level – class teachers;
- fourth level – parents.

The strategy rightly identifies the leadership of the head teacher in order to allow the co-ordinator to receive the necessary training prior to working with other staff on their curriculum area. This is clearly identified as an ongoing process and not a one-off event for the co-ordinator, and it should feed into their continuing professional development. This chapter only provides a taste of the different ways in which the head teacher could work with colleagues on developing the role.

The size of the school can make development much more complex. The small school, in which teachers have several subjects to co-ordinate, requires very careful prioritising and control so as not to overload the staff and the individual co-ordinators. The larger school may have the luxury of teachers who have only one subject to co-ordinate, but there are more teachers to monitor and more teachers from whom to obtain consensus.

Suggestions for the reader

1. Whatever your status, the role of the co-ordinator in school needs to be addressed as a whole-school issue. What procedures are in place for developing the co-ordinator's role in your school? Is there a monitoring policy or procedures for enabling monitoring to take place?

2. If you are a member of the senior management team within your school, what do you think you can do to develop the co-ordinating role?

12

Conclusions – what next?

Now you should have a clearer perspective of the role of the co-ordinator and of the potential of effective co-ordination, as well as of the difficulties. You should be in a position to identify the factors that you will need to influence in your school in order to be an effective co-ordinator. You will realise that co-ordination is a continuous process. You will need to return to the analysis of your role as a co-ordinator throughout your career. Your notebook will be a source of ideas and potential areas for future development. If you are particularly interested in looking at your role further, references to material that we drew on in the course of this book follow and may help you. Following on from that, you will find a reading list detailing other material which you may find helpful in your future work as a co-ordinator.

This book can only be a starting point, as all schools are different and it is therefore not possible to be prescriptive about the right way in which to do things. What works in one school may be a complete disaster in another. I hope that you will be able to adapt the ideas contained in this book to assist you in your role as co-ordinator, whether you are an experienced teacher or someone just entering the profession.

Suggestions for the reader

1. Maintain your file of your work, ideas and comments on in-service attended.

2. Continue to seek support in developing your role, through courses, reading, and feedback from colleagues, both informally and through the appraisal process.

Further reading

General reading for co-ordinators and specialists

ALEXANDER, R (1992), *Policy and practice in primary education*, London: Routledge.

ASSOCIATION OF TEACHERS AND LECTURERS (1993), *Eating the elephant bit by bit*, London: ATL.

BLENKINSOP, M (1991), 'Curriculum co-ordination, formal and informal rules: the role of the cross-school consultant', *Management in education*, Vol 5, No 2, Summer, pp2–3.

CAMPBELL, RJ (1984), 'In-school development: the role of the curriculum post holder', *School organisation*, Vol 4, No 4, pp345–57.

DONLAN, D (1983), 'The ordeal of in-service education: confessions of a paranoid consultant', *English journal*, Vol 72, No 4, April, pp30–2.

FOSTER, D, MAY, M AND BRACEWELL, M (1987), 'Curriculum leadership in primary education', *British journal of physical education*, Vol 18, No 4, July–August.

FULLAN, M (1982), *The meaning of educational change*, Toronto: OISE Press.

GODLEY, LB *et al* (1987), 'The teacher consultant role: impact on the profession', *Action in teacher education*, Vol 3, No 4, Winter, pp65–73.

HARGREAVES, DH AND HOPKINS, D (1991), *The empowered school: the management and practice of development planning*, London: Cassell Educational Ltd.

HARRISON, M (ed) (1994), *Beyond the core curriculum: co-ordinating the other foundation subjects in primary schools*, Plymouth: Northcote House.

KENNARD, J AND CARTER, D (1989b), 'Role expectation for curriculum co-ordinators', *Curriculum*, Vol 10, No 3, Winter, pp168–74.

MCMULLEN, R (1986), 'Curriculum co-ordination in the primary school: the background to one authority's programme for supporting the sharing of curricular expertise', *Inspection and advice*, Vol 21, No 2, Spring, pp15–17.

METROPOLITAN BOROUGH OF STOCKPORT (1984), *Specialisms in the primary school*, Metropolitan Borough of Stockport.

MORRISON, K (1985a), 'Tensions in subject-specialist teaching in the primary school', *Curriculum*, Vol 6, No 2, pp24–9.

PRIMARY SCHOOLS RESEARCH AND DEVELOPMENT GROUP (1983), *Curriculum responsibility and the use of teacher expertise in the primary school*, University of Birmingham School of Education.

RODGER, I *et al* (1983), *Teachers with posts of responsibility in primary schools*, University of Durham School of Education.

THORNTON, M (1990), 'Primary specialism', *Early years*, Vol 11, No 1, Autumn, pp34–9.

UNIVERSITY OF BIRMINGHAM (1983), *Curriculum responsibility and the use of teacher expertise in the primary school*, University of Birmingham Department of Curriculum Studies.

VISSER, J (1993), *Differentiation: making it work, ideas for staff development*, Stafford: NASEN Enterprises Ltd.

WATER, D (1983), *Responsibility and promotion in the primary school*, London: Heinemann.

Running in-service

CAMPBELL, RJ (1985), *Developing the primary school curriculum*, London: Holt, Rhinehart and Winston (especially Chs 5, 7, and 9).

CLIFT, P *et al* (1987), *Studies in school self-evaluation*, London: Falmer Press (especially Chs 1–3).

EASEN, P (1985), *Making school-centred INSET work*, Milton Keynes: Open University Press/Croom Helm.

ELLIOT, J (1983), 'Self-evaluation, professional development and accountability', in Galton, M (ed), *Changing school: changing curriculum*, London: Harper & Row.

FULLAN, M (1982), *The meaning of educational change*, Toronto: OISE Press (especially Chs 2, 3, 5, 6, 7 and 9).

GALTON, M (ed), *Changing school: changing curriculum*, Harper & Row.

GUBA, EG (1981), *Effective evaluation*, San Francisco, CA: Jossey Bass.

HANDY, C (1984), *Taken for granted: understanding schools as organisations*, Harlow: Longman.

REEVES, G (1995), 'Running an INSET session', *Primary file*, No 25, pp41–4.

RODGER, IA (1985), *Self-evaluation in primary schools*, London: Hodder & Stoughton.

SIMONS, H (1987), *Getting to know schools in a democracy*, London: Falmer Press.

SKELTON, M (1995), 'Schemes of work', *Primary file*, No 25, pp35–7.

SKILBECK, M (ed) (1984), *Evaluating the curriculum in the 80s*, London: Hodder & Stoughton (especially Chs 4, 5, 6, 7).

VISSER, J (1993), *Differentiation: making it work, ideas for staff development*, Stafford: NASEN Enterprises Ltd.

Books about the process of change

BLENKIN, GM AND KELLY, AV (eds) (1983), *The primary curriculum in action: a process approach to educational practice*, London: Harper & Row.

HOPKINS, D (1986), 'The change process and leadership in schools', *School organisation*, Vol 6, No 1, pp81–100.

HUSTLER, D (ed) (1986), *Action research in classrooms and schools*, London: Allen and Unwin.

SARASON, S (1982), *The culture of the school and the problem of change*, London: Allyn and Bacan.

Subject-specific reading for co-ordinators

English

DEPARTMENT OF EDUCATION AND SCIENCE (1975), *A Language for life* (Bullock Report), London: HMSO.

McCABE, PP (1990), 'The reading teacher as a workplace literacy consultant, reading', *Horizons*, Vol 31, No 1, October, pp14–21.

NATHAN, R (1991), 'Curriculum change: one consultant's perspective', *Creative word processing in the classroom*, Vol 8, No 3, January–February 1991, pp4–6.

NATIONAL WRITING PROJECT (1990), *Making changes – resources for INSET*, Walton-on-Thames: National Writing Project/Nelson.

Mathematics

BIGGS, E (1983), *Confident maths teaching, 5 to 13: INSET in the classroom*, Slough: NFER-Nelson

DEFORGES, C AND COCKBURN, A (1987), *Understanding the maths teacher: a study of practice in the first school*, London: Paul Chapman Publishing Ltd.

DEPARTMENT OF EDUCATION AND SCIENCE (1982), *Mathematics counts* (Cockcroft Report) (especially paragraphs 345–8), London: HMSO.

DEPARTMENT OF EDUCATION AND SCIENCE (1989b), *HMI reports on mathematics*, London: HMSO.

HARLING, P (1981), 'The primary school maths co-ordinator, *Maths in schools*, Vol 10, No 4, September, pp23–4.

INNER LONDON EDUCATION AUTHORITY (ILEA) (1988), *Mathematics in ILEA primary schools, part 2: Making it happen: a handbook for mathematics co-ordinators*, Leeds: AMS Educational.

NATIONAL CURRICULUM COUNCIL (1993), *Maths programmes of study: INSET for key stage 1 and 2*, London: HMSO.

OPEN UNIVERSITY STUDY PACK: *Supporting primary mathematics* (PM649G), Buckingham.

OPEN UNIVERSITY STUDY PACK: *Working together: school-based professional development in maths* (PM628), Buckingham.

PINDER, MT AND SHUARD, H (1985), *In-service education in primary maths*, Oxford: Oxford University Press.

SKILLING, D (1989), *Managing maths in the primary school*, Slough: NFER-Nelson.

STOW, M AND FOXMAN, D (1989), 'Mathematics co-ordination: study of practice in primary and middle schools', *Educational Research*, Vol 31, No 2, NFER, pp83–97.

WINTERIDGE, D (ed) (1989), *A handbook for primary maths co-ordinators*, London: Paul Chapman Publishing Ltd.

Physical education

BENTLEY, J (1985), 'The role of the post-holder in developing a school policy for physical education', *Primary teaching*, Vol 1, No 1, pp2–7.

EASTWOOD, P AND BUSHWELL, J (1987), 'Education and training for leadership in physical education', *Bulletin of physical education*, Vol 23, No 2, pp35–7.

FOSTER, D, MAY, M AND BRACEWELL, M (1987), 'Curriculum leadership in primary education', *British journal of physical education*, Vol 18, No 4, July–August.

WILLIAMSON, T *et al* (1984), 'Curriculum leadership in physical education', *Bulletin of physical education*, Vol 20, No 3, pp16–26.

Humanities

DAVIES, J (1994), 'The history co-ordinator's tale', in Harrison, M (ed), *Beyond the core curriculum: co-ordinating the other foundation subjects in primary schools*, Plymouth: Northcote House (Chapter 4).

HARRISON, M (ed) (1994), *Beyond the core curriculum: co-ordinating the other foundation subjects in primary schools*, Plymouth: Northcote House.

RAINEY, D AND KRAUSE, J (1994), 'The geography co-ordinator in primary school' in *ibid* (Chapter 6).

Science

BROWN, C AND WILSON, A (1983), 'Support for school-based curriculum development: the Cumbria Primary Science Project', *In-service Education*, Vol 9, No 3, Spring, pp162–7.

COMMONWEALTH ASSOCIATION OF SCIENCE, TECHNOLOGY AND MATHS EDUCATORS (1987), 'Co-ordinated science curriculum to age 16', *CASTME Journal*, Vol 7, No 2, pp19–21.

DEPARTMENT OF EDUCATION AND SCIENCE (1984), *Science in the primary school*, London: HMSO.

FROST, J AND TURNER, S (1988), 'Reflections on DES course for science co-ordinators in primary schools', *Primary science review*, No 5, Autumn, pp12–15.

NATIONAL CURRICULUM COUNCIL (1991), *Science and pupils with special educational needs*, York: NCC.

NATIONAL CURRICULUM COUNCIL (1993), *Teaching science at key stages 1 and 2*, York: NCC.

NEWTON, LD (1987), 'Co-ordinating science in a small primary school', *Primary science*, No 4, Summer.

OPEN UNIVERSITY PACK, *Issues in primary science* (PS548L).

SHERRINGTON, R (ed) (1993), *ASE science teachers' handbook – primary*, Hemel Hempsted: Simon and Schuster.

WALKINSON, A (1992), 'Subject specialism in primary schools', *Education in science*, ASE, No 150, November 1992, pp7–9.

Technology

HORRIDGE, S (1990), 'Co-ordinating technology: school perspective', *Modus*, April, pp83–7.

NEWTON, DP (1991), 'The role of the technology co-ordinator', *Primary teaching studies*, Vol 6, No 2, October, pp129–36.

NEWTON, S (1983), 'Policies on educational technology, regional co-ordination by local education authorities: the case for regional co-ordination', *Education*, Vol 162, No 17, October 1983, p327.

Modern foreign languages

CRISPIN, A (1986), 'Co-ordinated resources for modern languages (CORM), *Modern languages in Scotland*, No 30, August 1986, pp35–42.

Music

SANDY, A AND BRIT, J (1988), 'Music consultancy in primary education', *Music education*, Vol 5, No 3, November 1988, pp217–40.

Health education

O'CONNOR, L (1991), 'Developing health education in the primary school: review', *Early child development and care*, Vol 66, No 91, pp145–62.

Special educational needs

BUTT, N (1991), 'A role for SEN co-ordinators in the 1990s: a reply to Syson', *Support for learning*, Vol 6, No 1, February 1991, p15.
DYSON, A (1990), 'Effective learning consultancy: a future role for special needs co-ordinators?' *Support for learning*, Vol 5, No 3, August 1990, pp116–27.

References

ALEXANDER, R (1984), *Primary teaching*, London: Holt, Rhinehart and Winston.

ALEXANDER, R (1991), *Primary education in Leeds: briefing and summary*, Leeds: University of Leeds.

BELB (1990), *Differentiated provision in secondary schools*, Belfast Education and Library Board.

BENNETT, B AND KELL, J (1989), *A good start: four-year-olds in infant schools*, Oxford: Basil Blackwell.

BENTLEY, J (1985), 'The role of the post-holder in developing a school policy for physical education', *Primary teaching*, Vol 1, No 1, pp2–7.

BRENNAN, WJ (1985), *Curriculum for special needs*, Buckingham: Open University Press.

CALDERHEAD, J (1984), *Teachers' classroom decision making*, London: Holt, Rhinehart and Winston.

CAMPBELL, RJ (1985), *Developing the primary school curriculum*, London: Holt, Rinehart and Winston.

CENTRAL ADVISORY COUNCIL FOR EDUCATION (CACE) (ENGLAND) (1967), *Children and their primary schools (Plowden Report)*, London: HMSO.

CROSS, A AND CROSS, S (1994), 'Organising a professional development day for your colleagues', in Harrison, M (ed), *Beyond the core curriculum*, Plymouth: Northcote House (Chapter 3).

CURRICULUM COUNCIL FOR WALES (CCW) (1990), *Economic and industrial understanding: a framework for the development of a cross-curricular theme in Wales*, Advisory Paper 7, Cardiff, CCW.

CURRICULUM COUNCIL FOR WALES (CCW) (1991a), *Community understanding: a framework for the development of a cross-curricular theme in Wales*, Advisory Paper 11, Cardiff, CCW.

CURRICULUM COUNCIL FOR WALES (CCW) (1991b), *The whole curriculum 5–16 in Wales: principles and issues for consideration by schools in curriculum planning and implementation*, Cardiff, CCW.

CURRICULUM COUNCIL FOR WALES (CCW) (1991c), *Health education: introducing health education as a cross-curricular theme*, Bulletin 4, Cardiff, CCW/Youth Life Wales.

DAVIES, J (1994), 'The history co-ordinator's tale', in Harrison, M (ed), *Beyond the core curriculum*, Plymouth: Northcote House (Chapter 4).

DEARDEN, R (1968), *The philosophy of primary education: an introduction*, London: Routledge and Kegan Paul.

DEPARTMENT OF EDUCATION AND SCIENCE (1975), *A language for life (Bullock Report),* London: HMSO.

DEPARTMENT OF EDUCATION AND SCIENCE (1978a), *Primary education in England: a survey by HM Inspectors of Schools,* London: HMSO.

DEPARTMENT OF EDUCATION AND SCIENCE (1982a), *Education 5–9: an illustrative survey of 80 first schools in England,* London: HMSO.

DEPARTMENT OF EDUCATION AND SCIENCE (1982), *Mathematics Counts (Cockroft Report),* London: HMSO.

DEPARTMENT OF EDUCATION AND SCIENCE (1984), *Science in the primary school,* London: HMSO.

DEPARTMENT OF EDUCATION AND SCIENCE (1985), *The curriculum from 5–16: the responses to curriculum matters 2,* an HMI series, London: HMSO.

DEPARTMENT OF EDUCATION AND SCIENCE (1987), *School teachers' pay and conditions of employment,* London: HMSO, March 1987.

DEPARTMENT OF EDUCATION AND SCIENCE (1989b), *HMI reports on mathematics,* London: HMSO.

DEPARTMENT FOR EDUCATION (1992), *Guidance on audits of teaching staff,* London: HMSO.

DEPARTMENT FOR EDUCATION (1992), *Curriculum organisation and classroom practice in primary schools: a discussion paper,* London: HMSO.

DEPARTMENT FOR EDUCATION (1993a), *Curriculum organisation and classroom practice in primary schools: a follow-up report,* London, HMSO.

FOSTER, D, MAY, M AND BRACEWELL, M (1987), 'Curriculum leadership in primary education', *British journal of physical education,* Vol 18, No 4, July–August.

FULLAN, M (1982), *The meaning of educational change,* Toronto: OISE Press.

GALTON, M, SIMON, B AND CROLL, P (1980), *Inside the primary classroom,* London: Routledge and Kegan Paul.

HARRIS, D AND BELL, C (1990), *Evaluating and assessing for learning,* London: Routledge and Kegan Paul.

HARRISON, M (ed) (1994), *Beyond the core curriculum; co-ordinating the other foundation subjects in primary schools,* Plymouth: Northcote House.

HARRISON, M AND CROSS, A (1994), 'Successful curriculum change through co-ordination', in Harrison, M (ed), *Beyond the core curriculum,* Plymouth: Northcote House (Chapter 2).

HARRISON, S AND THEAKER, K (1989), *Curriculum leadership and co-ordination in the primary school,* Whalley, Lancs: Guild House Press.

HIRST, PH (1965), 'Liberal education and the nature of knowledge', in Archenbault, RD (ed), *Philosophical analysis and education,* London: Routledge and Kegan Paul.

HIRST, P AND PETERS, RS (1970), *The logic of education,* London: Routledge and Kegan Paul.

HORRIDGE, S (1990), 'Co-ordinating technology: school perspective', *Modus,* April, pp83–7.

HOUSE OF COMMONS EDUCATION COMMITTEE (1994), Disparity in funding between primary and secondary schools, London: HMSO.

House of Commons Parliamentary Papers, 1985–6, London: Chadwyck Healey.

INNER LONDON EDUCATION AUTHORITY (ILEA) (1988), *Mathematics in ILEA primary schools, part 2: Making it happen: a handbook for mathematics co-ordinators,* Leeds: AMS Educational.

LACEY, C (1970), *Hightown Grammar, Manchester,* Manchester: Manchester University Press.

MILLER, A (1989), 'Towards a work-related curriculum', *SCIP news*, 25, Winter, University of Warwick: Schools Curriculum Industry Partnership/Mini Enterprise in Schools Project.

MORRISON, K (1985a), 'Tensions in subject-specialist teaching in the primary school', *Curriculum*, Vol 6, No 2, pp24–9.

MORRISON, K AND RIDLEY, K (1988), *Curriculum planning and the primary school*, London: Paul Chapman Publishing Ltd.

MORTIMORE, P, SAMMONS, P, STOLL, L, LEWIS, D AND ECOB, R (1988), *School matters: the junior years*, Frome, Somerset: Open Books.

MUSCHAMP, Y, JONES, A, MORTIMORE, A, PARKER-REES, R, POLLARD, W, ROBERTS, D, THYER, J, WILSON, W AND POLLARD, A (1991), *Practical issues in primary education Number 8: pupil self-assessment*, Bristol: National Primary Centre (South West) and County of Avon Public Relations and Publicity.

NATIONAL CURRICULUM COUNCIL (1989), *Curriculum guidance: a framework for the primary curriculum*, York: NCC.

NATIONAL CURRICULUM COUNCIL (1990a), *Curriculum guidance 3: the whole curriculum*, York: NCC.

NATIONAL CURRICULUM COUNCIL (1990b), *Curriculum guidance 4: education for economic and industrial understanding*, York: NCC.

NATIONAL CURRICULUM COUNCIL (1990c), *Curriculum guidance 5: health education*, York: NCC.

NATIONAL CURRICULUM COUNCIL (1990d), *Curriculum guidance 6: careers education and guidance*, York: NCC.

NATIONAL CURRICULUM COUNCIL (1990e), *Curriculum guidance 7: environmental education*, York: NCC.

NATIONAL CURRICULUM COUNCIL (1990f), *Curriculum guidance 8: education for citizenship*, York: NCC.

NATIONAL CURRICULUM COUNCIL (1991), *Science and pupils with special educational needs*, York: NCC.

NATIONAL CURRICULUM COUNCIL (1993), *Teaching science at key stages 1 and 2*, York: NCC.

NATIONAL WRITING PROJECT (1990), *Making changes – resources for INSET*, Walton-on-Thames: National Writing Project/Nelson.

NEWTON, DP (1991), 'The role of the technology co-ordinator', *Primary teaching studies*, Vol 6, No 2, October, pp129–36.

NEWTON, LD (1987), 'Co-ordinating science in a small primary school', *Primary science*, No 4, Summer.

NIAS, J (1989), *Primary teachers talking: a study of teaching as work*, London: Routledge.

NIAS, J, SOUTHWARK, G AND YEOMANS, R (1989), *Staff relationships in the primary school: a study of organisational cultures*, London: Cassell.

NORWICH, B (1990), *Special needs in ordinary schools*, London: Cassell.

OFFICE FOR STANDARDS IN EDUCATION (OFSTED) (1993), *Handbook for the inspection of schools*, London: HMSO.

OFFICE FOR STANDARDS IN EDUCATION (OFSTED) (1995a), *Teaching quality: the primary debate. A report on Ofsted conferences*, London: HMSO.

OFFICE FOR STANDARDS IN EDUCATION (OFSTED) (1995b), *Handbook: Guidance on the inspection of nursery and primary schools*, London: HMSO.

OPEN UNIVERSITY, E628, *English in the primary curriculum: developing reading and writing*, October 1992, Buckingham.

OPEN UNIVERSITY, E624, *Planning learning in the primary curriculum*, October 1993, Buckingham.

POLLARD, A (1985), *The social world of the primary school*, London: Cassell Educational Ltd.

POLLARD, A AND TANN, S (1987), *Reflective teaching in the primary school*, London: Cassell Educational Ltd.

PRIMARY SCHOOLS RESEARCH AND DEVELOPMENT GROUP (1983), *Curriculum responsibility and the use of teacher expertise in the primary school*, University of Birmingham School of Education.

PRING, R (1976), *Curriculum design and development*, Buckingham: Open University Press.

RAINEY, D AND KRAUSE, J (1994), 'The geography co-ordinator in primary school', in Harrison, M (ed), *Beyond the core curriculum*, Plymouth: Northcote House (Chapter 6).

RICHARDS, C (1988), 'Primary education in England: an analysis of some recent issues and developments', in Clarkson, M (ed) (1988), *Emerging issues in primary education*, London: Falmer Press.

SCHOOLS COUNCIL (1983), *Teachers with posts of responsibility in primary schools. Programme one*, University of Durham.

SCHOOLS COUNCIL (PRIMARY SCHOOLS RESEARCH AND DEVELOPMENT GROUP) (1984), *Curriculum responsibility and teacher expertise in the primary schools – five studies*, University of Birmingham.

SHIPMAN, M (1979), *In-school evaluation*, London: Heinemann Educational.

SIMPSON, M (1989), *A study of differentiation and learning in primary schools*, Aberdeen: Northern College of Education.

SKELTON, M (1995), 'Schemes of work', *Primary file*, No 25, pp35–7.

STOW, M AND FOXMAN, D (1989), 'Mathematics co-ordination: study of practice in primary and middle schools', *Educational research*, Vol 31, No 2, NFER, pp83–97.

SWANN, W (1988), 'Learning difficulties and the curriculum: reform, integration or differentiation', in Thomas, G and Fieler, A (eds), *Planning for special needs*, Oxford: Basil Blackwell.

THORNTON, M (1990), 'Primary specialism', *Early years*, Autumn, Vol 11, No 1, pp34–9.

TIZARD, B, BLATCHFORD, P, BURKE, J, FAQUER, C AND LEWIS, I (1988), *Young children at school in the inner city*, London and Hove: Lawrence Erlbaum Associates.

VISSER, J (1993), *Differentiation: making it work, ideas for staff development*, Stafford: NASEN Enterprises Ltd.

WEBB (1993), *Eating the elephant bit by bit* (report commissioned by the Association of Teachers and Lecturers), London: ATL.

WESTON, P (1992), 'A decade for differentiation', *British journal of special education*, Vol 19, No 1, pp6–9.

WILLIAMSON, T et al (1984), 'Curriculum leadership in physical education', *Bulletin of physical education*, Vol 20, No 3, pp16–26.

YOUNG, MFD (ed) (1971), *Knowledge and control: new directions for the sociology of education*, London: Collier-Macmillan.